beatty's cabin

by

ELLIOTT S. BARKER

Order this book online at www.trafford.com
or email orders@trafford.com

Most Trafford titles are also available at major online book retailers.

Printed in the United States of America.

ISBN: 978-1-4269-6059-8 (sc)
ISBN: 978-1-4269-6060-4 (hc)
ISBN: 978-1-4269-6061-1 (e)

Library of Congress Control Number: 2011904679

Trafford rev. 04/19/2011

 www.trafford.com

North America & international
toll-free: 1 888 232 4444 (USA & Canada)
phone: 250 383 6864 ◆ fax: 812 355 4082

beatty's cabin

Adventures in the Pecos High Country

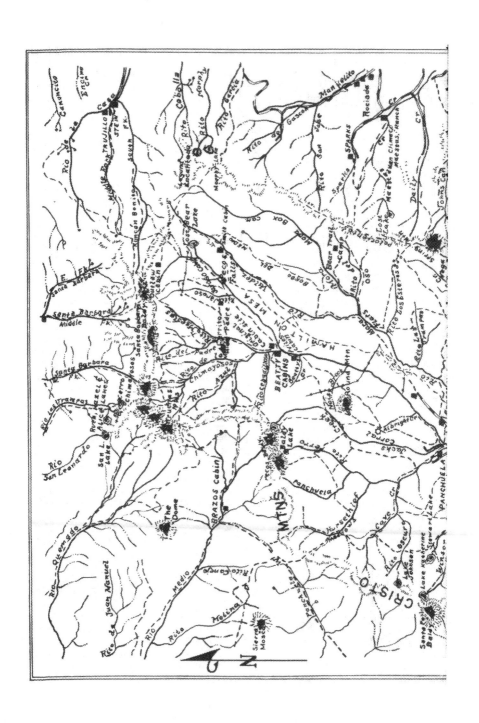

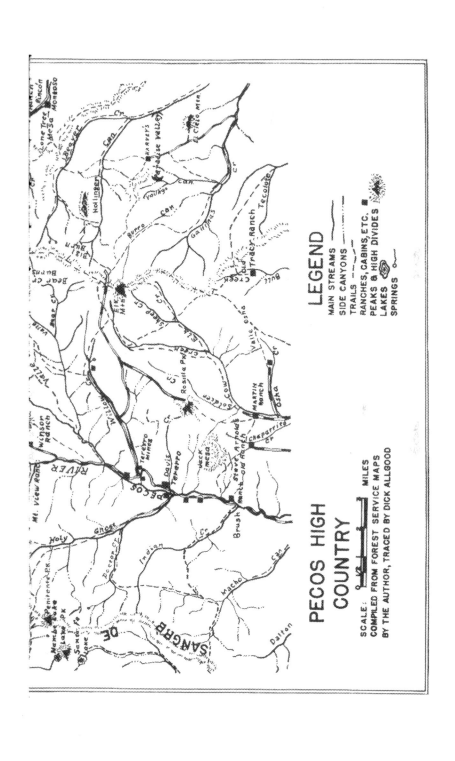

PECOS HIGH
COUNTRY

SCALE: |___|___|___| MILES
COMPILED FROM FOREST SERVICE MAPS
BY THE AUTHOR, TRACED BY DICK ALLGOOD

LEGEND

MAIN STREAMS ————
SIDE CANYONS ————
TRAILS - - - - - -
RANCHES, CABINS, ETC. ■
PEAKS & HIGH DIVIDES ❋
LAKES ◈
SPRINGS ∿

to ethel

Who, after fifty-nine years,
Three children, ten grandchildren and
Eleven great grandchildren,
Still loves to pack back into the beautiful
Pecos high country with me to fish for trout
And to camp beneath a canopy of drooping spruce
Boughs at the edge of some pristine,
Flower-spangled park.

acknowledgments

Acknowledgment is made to Norman Appleton, Santa Fe artist, for the dust jacket painting.

The Author makes grateful acknowledgment for permission to quote from *Breaking New Ground,* by Gifford Pinchot (Har-court, Brace and Company, 1947), and to use pictures and quotations from *Camp Fires of a Naturalist,* by Clarence E. Edwords (D. Appleton and Company, 1893).

Appreciation is extended also to S. Omar Barker, J. W. Johnson, and Harold Walter for the privilege of quoting their peak-climbing stories; to Frank Wesner, Bob Ground, F. M. Wynkoop, and others for valuable contributions of material; to Harold Walter for many excellent pictures, including the picture (minus the cabin) from which the jacket painting was made; to the New Mexico Tourist Bureau and the U. S. Forest Service for some fine pictures; and to Dorothy Harvey and Edna Fetterman for old Harvey Ranch pictures; to Mrs. L. L. Dyche for picture and valuable data; to S. Omar Barker and Elsa Barker for technical advice; and to May Walter for typing of manuscript.

The Author also wishes to express deep appreciation to the many others who have been of assistance in the compilation of factual data for these stories.

2011

As Elliott Barker's heirs (grandchildren and great grandchildren), we are extremely proud to republish "Beatty's Cabin" so that future generations can be inspired by his "adventures and tales". He was a great story teller and conservationist long before it was popular to be one.

preface

Despite the chill November night, the iron cook stove in the corner of Beatty's Cabin kept the room cozy. Two big, soft, gray elk hides were draped over the yard fence, while eight quarters of fresh red meat hung under the shed back of the cabin. An unusually fine set of twelve-point elk antlers leaned against the outside of the log cabin, where the saddles hung. Two successful hunters were proudly happy, the other three hopeful for tomorrow.

We had eaten our fill of fresh elk liver and bacon, hot biscuits, milk gravy, and French fried potatoes. The two lucky nimrods had told and retold their exciting experiences of the day. Then, perhaps prodded a little, I had unwound a few tales of the many thrilling events of the area since the old-time prospector, George Beatty, built his two-room log cabin on the little grassy flat across the creek right here in the heart of this primitive Pecos high country about eighty years ago.

I had told them of my own first pack trip to Beatty's Cabin as a ten-year-old boy, way back in 1896; about George Beatty and his "sure good bear knives"; about naturalist L. L. Dyche's hunting excursion after grizzly bear among these very canyons and ridges; about Dyche's strange honeymoon trip to Beatty's Cabin with his timid, diminutive Kansas bride, sixty-nine years ago; about the discovery of an outlaw cabin at the head of the river and capture of the outlaws; about the bishop-raised Indian, Miguel Lamy, getting mauled and chewed up by a bear, but finally killing it with a butcher knife; and about the perilous winter rescue of a bunch of snow-trapped horses.

They might have kept my tongue wagging all night but, having helped to dress and pack in the big bull elk, I was, perhaps, more tired than the younger men. At last, I said, "You guys can sit up all night throwing the 'bull' if you like; I'm going to bed."

"Elliott, stories such as those ought to be in a book," Angus said, "Why don't you write it?"

"Not tonight! But maybe I'll find time to try it some day," I replied.

"What will you call it?" asked Bill. "Hell in the High Country?"

"Not exactly," I said. "Anyway naming a book before it is written might be like naming an unborn child John Henry; it might have to be changed to Mary Jane."

All the same, I knew right then that the title would have to come to me out of my many fond memories of the area.

"This spot is the hub of the Pecos Wilderness area, finest mountain country anywhere," I said, "for a century or more, the pivotal axis for thrilling experiences and rugged adventures, many happy, a few tragic. With salty horse-sweat stinging my crotch from riding behind a pack saddle, I got my own first inspiring glimpse of the remote Pecos high country. On that very same adventuresome trip, I explored Beatty's old cabin and prospect holes. Scores of times since then, while on all sorts of missions, I have camped right here at Beatty's Cabin—and that's my title: simply BEATTY'S CABIN."

So it was on a frosty hunters' night, with the babble of the upper Pecos water and the whispers in our ears of mountain breezes among the spruces, that a book came into being, nebulous at first, but taking form gradually, chapter by chapter, until this outdoorsman's volume is humbly offered for your entertainment—and approval—I hope.

contents

I

cabin in the
wilderness

George Beatty, like many other pioneer prospectors, never struck it rich. When I was a boy, around the turn of the century, I knew him fairly well. At that time he had some prospect holes over near Harvey's resort, six miles south of our mountain ranch, and some similar interests near Rociada, a few miles to the north. While traveling afoot, with a pack burro, back and forth through the country he sometimes stayed over night or longer at our ranch home in the northern New Mexico Mountains.

We kids thought his distinctive mustache and little goatee ridiculous and funny, but we listened wide eyed to his wild tales of adventures in the mountains and how he had so often been on the verge of striking a gold mine. Ma and Pa were patiently tolerant of his outlandish stories, which he seemed to think were necessary to reciprocate for the hospitality he enjoyed.

He sometimes spoke of his cabin on the upper Pecos River, referring to it as his "ranch," but by then, I am sure, he had completely abandoned it. The cabin was situated about •eighteen miles from our place on Sapello Creek, and lay on the opposite side of the rugged east prong of the southern end of the Sangre de Cristo Mountains, which we always referred to as the Main Range.

But there is a much earlier authentic account of George Beatty, his goatee, his foot-long bear knives, his story-telling, flavored with typical mountaineer profanity, and of his cabin on the upper Pecos. This record I find in a prized old book, titled *Camp Fires of a Naturalist,* which has been

1

out of print for more than fifty years. The book was written by Clarence E. Ed-words, from the notes and diaries of L. L. Dyche, a naturalist who made three excursions into the northern New Mexico Mountains in the early 1880's for the University of Kansas, at Lawrence, Kansas. Professor Dyche's activities were centered around Montezuma, Harvey's Ranch, and the upper Pecos, and he came in quest of specimens of insects and birds, whitetail and mule deer, elk, black and grizzly bear, and other mammals indigenous to the region.

According to the record, George Beatty then had a mica mine near Harvey's Ranch, atop a mountain twenty-eight miles west of Las Vegas. (The thirty- to forty-foot shaft is still there unless someone has recently cut it up for post holes). He was also doing some prospecting on the headwaters of the Pecos River, where he had built a little, two-roomed log cabin on a little grassy flat below a ledge of rock between the main, or Falls, fork and the west, or Rito del Padre, fork of the Pecos River. Just why this site was selected is not known, but it could be simply that its wondrous beauty found response in the heart of this lonely wanderer of the wilderness. While no mineral discovery was ever made in the vicinity, the old prospect holes where Beatty dug into a vein of quartz walled by mica schist, near the cabin site, may still be seen today.

When I first saw the cabin, more than a half century ago, it had been abandoned and the dirt roof was beginning to cave in. Now there is left only a little heap of earth and stone where the fireplace once stood. But the place is still known as "Beatty's Cabin" and it is the most noted spot in the entire Pecos Wilderness area, now having come to mean the general locality. A hunter or a fisherman may say he is packing into Beatty's Cabin, yet pitch his tent anywhere within a radius of two or three miles of the spot where the cabin stood. The U. S. Forest Service and State Game Department administrative cabins, now located just across the creek, also are referred to as Beatty's Cabin.

The naturalist, Professor L. L. Dyche, made two consecutive summer excursions into this general region and had some thrilling and hair-raising experiences with grizzly bear, which will be touched on in a later chapter. On those two trips there is no record that he visited Beatty's Cabin, but on his third trip, in 1884, after missing one year, he brought his bride, a timid Kansas girl, with him to Harvey's Ranch and from there on burro-back to Beatty's Cabin.

Harvey's Ranch was christened Paradise Valley by H. A. Harvey, retired Boston merchant, who homesteaded there in 1881. The valley consists of some big, beautiful mountain parks and meadows near the top of the mountain which lies between Hollinger Canyon, on the north, and Gallinas Creek, on the south. At the base of the mountain, seven miles below, Mr. Harvey had a carriage house, and from that point to Las Vegas, twenty-one miles to the east, travel was by horse-drawn wagons and carriages. But from the carriage house to Paradise Valley there was only a steep saddle-trail, and all travel and transportation were by horseback or burro-back.

The affable and enterprising Mr. Harvey, with his charming wife, Rhea, soon turned their little ranch into a unique log cabin summer resort which flourished for years. Vacationists, both local and those from the East, were always delighted with the jolly seven-mile trip up the steep, pine-clad mountain burro-back. They were charmed by the feeling of remoteness and inaccessibility of the beautiful, wild valley, and invigorated by the cool, rare atmosphere found at the elevation of nearly ten thousand feet. It was truly a wilderness paradise.

The burro saddle-and-pack train often numbered as many as thirty animals on the regular weekly trips to the carriage house during summer months. One set of guests would be taken down the mountain burro-back and on to Las Vegas by carriage one day, and the next day another group would be brought back. There were very gentle burros for novices and for children big enough to ride alone. For babies, from six months up to three or four years, there was Old Reuben, a big, gray, floppy-eared burro, as sure-footed and trustworthy an animal as ever lived, on whose back in two special pack-boxes the children would be secured for the trip up the mountain. If there were two youngsters, one would be securely lodged in each box; if only one, groceries in the other box would balance the load.

While mothers were sometimes reluctant to entrust their offspring to a strange jackass, it may be recorded that in the thirty years that the resort operated there was never an accident on the trail—in gratifying contrast to the gory highway traffic toll caused by jackasses today.

Finally, Mr. Harvey took in a partner who insisted upon building a road to the resort in Paradise Valley to make it easier of access. The road was not only costly to build but it quickly killed the resort business. The charm of the seven-mile trip up the mountain, on the back of a floppy-eared burro, to enjoy a glorious week end in the enchanted wilderness-meadow log cabin resort was lost completely when horse-drawn carriages began bumping guests over a dangerous mountain road. So would it be if, as some desire, the Pecos high country and other wilderness areas were made accessible by auto roads. Their inherent charm would vanish and be lost forever.

It was to that Paradise Valley atop the mountain, before it became a resort that Professor Dyche brought his young bride on their wedding trip. Mrs. Dyche's experience riding a burro up from the carriage house was aggravating but fun. The burro, though gentle, had a mind of his own and would take advantage of his inexperienced passenger by wandering off the trail to graze, despite the lady's efforts to keep him going. Then, when the other burros got out of sight, braying raucously, he would break into a lope to catch up.

At the ranch, Mrs. Dyche was delighted with the flower-spangled parks and meadows surrounded by white-barked, trembling-leafed aspens and stately spruce trees, and charmed by Mrs. Harvey's kindness and hospitality. In such a mood it was that she let her adventuresome husband talk her into making a trip with him and George Beatty to Beatty's Cabin. There, Beatty assured them, he had stored abundant supplies, with the best hunting and fishing in the world at his doorstep. Dyche knew full well what the trip would be like for it would lead them into the same rugged wilderness area where he had hunted grizzly bear on two previous trips, but Mrs. Dyche had little idea of the experiences of the wild in store for her.

The start was made early one morning with Mrs. Dyche on old Reuben, Beatty leading the way to pick out the very dim trail while Professor Dyche brought up the rear to haze the pack burros along. Soon all signs of a trail vanished and Beatty drew two huge knives, with blades a foot long, from his belt to cut away limbs and brush so the burro train could get through with packs and fair passenger.

According to Dyche's written account, Beatty flourished the big knives and boastfully said, "These are sure good bear knives and long enough to reach a bear's heart. I made them, too, out of a drill. If a bear ever comes across this old man he will sure feel these knives in his heart. See these here buck horn handles? Well, I sure made them, too, and I sure killed the buck that wore the horns."

Dyche had his own ideas as to what would happen in such an encounter with a grizzly, but he drew the mountaineer out until the woods rang with his big bear-talk. And so, as Beatty beguiled the way, despite a bride's tree-bumped knees, the day passed pleasantly enough for a trailless wilderness trip and a comfortable camp was made the first night, in a park by a spring near Elk Mountain.

The next day took them through some long, tedious stretches of burned and tangled fallen timber, where the burros caused much trouble by running into snags and tearing the packs. A camp site was reached at last, on the slope of a mountain near a bunch of aspen and spruce trees. As they approached the spot where camp was to be pitched, an old hen grouse flew up and soon her brood of young could be heard calling in the tall grass. Mrs. Dyche could not rest until she had diligently hunted for and, at last, found and caught the young birds. She then snuggled them under a blanket till morning, when they were released, spry and uninjured, to respond to the mother bird's continued calling nearby.

Late the third afternoon, when they were within a few rods of the cabin, the donkey train was halted and Dyche reports that Beatty exclaimed, "See that tree there? I met an old grizzly there. I had been fishing and sure had thirty fish on a stringer, not one of them less than a foot long, and was within thirty feet of a bear before I saw him. I sure shinned up that tree in a hurry, and the bear ate up every one of those fish and then licked the stringer. He then looked up at me and walked off about his business."

"Why didn't you kill him with your big bear knives?" Dyche asked.

"I had left my knives in the cabin or there sure would have been the darndest bear fight ever seen in these mountains."

At the cabin at last, they saw that, sure enough, a big bear had been there very recently. The little garden had been torn up and the huge tracks were everywhere.

"See?" exclaimed Beatty, "There are bears here, the woods are full of them."

Unlocking the door of the little, two-roomed log cabin, Beatty went in, and then bounced right out again popeyed with excitement.

"I've sure been robbed. Somebody's taken everything I had, even my gun and pistol. Ain't enough left for one meal. I'll follow them if it takes all my life and if I ever cross their trail they'll sure be mine!" exclaimed Beatty. He raved on all evening, flavoring his comments with many a high-powered mountaineer's oath. Dyche tried hard but was unsuccessful in quieting him down.

The timid bride, shocked beyond measure, retreated to the creek to contemplate the babbling brook, despite an abundance of fresh bear tracks all around. All night long Beatty kept up his profane tirade keeping the tired travelers of the wilderness awake. Next morning he set out afoot for the nearest ranch, twenty-five miles down the river in search of the robbers.

Beatty's constant talk of bears and the robbers, confirmed by evidence of both, and his oaths, which were all too real, were too much for the young bride. She decided she'd had enough. Her husband agreed that if, in reality, there were robbers around it might be wise to get out of this locality. They had brought along supplies enough to last them a week or ten days more, and the creeks were full of fish, and the forests full of deer. So, despite the fatigue of the three-day trip just completed, they set out on their back track soon after Beatty had left.

All the same, Beatty's Cabin had served one night as a bridal suite, despite robbers, mammoth bear tracks, and an old prospector's profanity.

They camped the first night on the return trip at Mora Flats, a beautiful mountain valley at the junction of Valdez and Mora creeks, where they and their pack animals got a good night's rest. Next day, instead of continuing on the back trail to Harvey's, they took a side trip to one of Dyche's earlier camps, which he had named Bear Trail Camp. Here they found everything in order just as it had been left two years before. Mrs. Dyche was now reassured enough to stay several days in this delightful spot, feasting on mountain trout and venison. It is recorded that they enjoyed their honeymoon stay at this camp in the wilderness better than if they had been at a fine summer hotel.

Bear Trail Camp is now called Rito del Oso, Spanish for Little Bear Creek, but, no doubt, it got its name from the naturalist's pioneer camp and adventures with fierce grizzlies there.

When Beatty arrived, still fuming, at a ranch way down the river he found that his old partner, Mr. Everhart, had heard that Beatty was sick in Las Vegas, and had sent a young man up to look after the cabin until he should return. Pestered by bears all about the place, the boy had got scared and buried all of Beatty's supplies, guns, and equipment in a hole under the puncheon floor of the cabin to keep them safe from bears and robbers, then made a bee line back to the ranch.

The chagrined Beatty's only comment was, "That kid sure knew his business. He sure did fool this old man."

A Remarkable Coincidence

After the foregoing pages had been written, I wrote to the University of Kansas to check on dates and other material in connection with Professor Dyche's work in the Pecos high country. The librarian replied that the information seemed not to be available in their records, but added, "Mrs. L. L. Dyche, at the age of 94, is still living here in Lawrence, alert mentally and physically, so I called her up and she gave me the information you wanted."

I was astounded, but greatly pleased-to learn that the lady who, as a bride sixty-nine years ago, made the burro-back trip into the trailless Pecos Wilderness area was still very much alive. I at once corresponded with Mrs. Dyche and her daughter, Miss Ruth O. Dyche, and made an appointment to go to see the little lady who made a honeymoon trip to Beatty's Cabin three score and eight years ago. Ordinarily, I would have more than a little difficulty in getting my wife's consent to go to see another woman, but in this instance, she magnanimously said to go ahead.

I found Mrs. L. L. Dyche to be a charming and gracious person, and when I asked her to go out and have dinner with me that evening, her eyes sparkled and she said, "Sure, I'll be happy to." Then, with gracious hospitality, she and Miss Dyche insisted that I spend the night at their home instead of going to a hotel.

Mrs. Dyche vividly recalled many of the characteristics of Old Reuben, who carried her through the wilderness. George Beatty and his cabin were well remembered, also.

In those days, it was not considered ladylike for a woman to ride astride or to wear trousers. I suspected that this little woman might have pioneered in changing that silly tradition. When asked whether she had worn a divided riding skirt or trousers, Mrs. Dyche hesitated a moment, then blushingly replied, "I am sure I didn't wear a skirt; the trousers I wore were probably borrowed from one of the teen-aged Harvey boys." So, sure enough, she had been a pioneer and adventurer in more ways than one. She recalled that the streams were full of trout, but wasn't sure whether she caught any or not.

It was learned that Professor Dyche, for many years curator of the Kansas University Museum, was chosen by the National Museum to head the expedition, in 1895, that rescued the Arctic explorer, Robert E. Peary, from the frozen north. He served also as State Game Warden of Kansas from 1909 until his death, in 1914, while' retaining his position at the University.

Miss Dyche accompanied me through the outstanding Museum of Natural History which her father worked so hard and loyally in the early days to build up. I was particularly interested because the Naturalist had obtained specimens of grizzly bear, black bear, deer, and other mammals and a great variety of birds from the Pecos high country when it was in a truly primitive state.

2

my first trip to beatty's cabin

My father's little mountain ranch lay well back in the Sangre de Cristo Mountains on Sapello Creek. Everywhere around the ranch house, on this memorable morning, there was feverish activity. Even before the sun had penetrated into the deeply shadowed canyon, Pa and my brother Charlie were out at the corral saddling the horses while my older sisters were getting the camp bedding ready on the porch. Ma was busy inside getting the camp utensils and grub together and fixing a half-dozen noon lunches. Everybody was busy, and excitedly happy—that is, everybody but me.

My spirits were lower than a grasshopper's chin. The folks and some of the neighbors were going on a camping trip into the Pecos high country and Pa wouldn't let me go along. "Shucks, you are only ten years old," he said. That made no impression at all on me, for I wanted, with all my heart and soul, to go anyway.

I was following Pa around a-bellerin' and a-blubberin' and constantly getting in the way and, all the while, pleading, as only a barefoot boy can, over and over between lachrymose sobs, "I wanta go! I wanta go!"

"I said you can't, so go on in the house and shut up," Pa scolded.

But I didn't go in the house and I didn't shut up either. At the risk of getting a good licking, I continued my plaintive "I wanta go! I wanta go, too!" while the sobs grew louder and the tears saltier.

I'll never know why, for Pa wasn't one to give in, once he had made up his mind, but, finally, when the big, bulky pack had been tied on old

9

Frances, to my everlasting joy, he said, "Consarn it, go on and ask your Ma; if she says you can go, all right."

Mother was a lot more sympathetic and I lost no time telling her what Pa had said and beseeching her to give her consent, also. At last, wiping my tear-begrimed face on her apron, she said, "I shouldn't let you go but I reckon you can."

I darted out the door so fast I stubbed my sore toe on a stick of firewood in the yard and fell down. I jumped up in a jiffy and, in my excitement, forgot to limp as I ran barefooted to the corral where Pa was. "Ma says I can, Ma says I can go," I yelled with utter delight.

"Then go get your shoes on, we are about ready to start; better get a coat, too."

Believe me, with Mother's help, I was ready in no time at all, and when I came out the neighbors who were going had just ridden up. There were not enough horses for me to have one of my own so I had to ride on old Frances' broad, bare hips, back of the big pack. That didn't matter at all—I was on my way to camp in the Pecos high country 1

That was fifty-six years ago and I don't rightly remember now just who made up the party. Pa and my older brother Charlie and, I think, two older sisters, Mr. Ground, a neighbor, and some of his family, perhaps Percy Crews, and some others. But there are many other details and incidents of the trip which greatly impressed me and which I remember as vividly as if they had happened last year.

Father and Mother, with their large family, had settled there on a mountain ranch in Sapello Canyon seven years before, and the country was still pretty wild, with but a few dim trails into the back country. Pa and some of the others had made several trips to the Pecos high country, where they found excellent trout fishing in the Mora, Valdez, and Pecos rivers. It was a kind of busman's holiday. Living, as we did, deep in the mountains on an excellent little trout stream, for our vacation we went even deeper into the mountains, where there were more and bigger trout streams.

Old Frances was a big, fifteen-hundred-pound work mare, pressed into service as a pack animal, I suppose, because she was very strong and could carry all our camp equipment, bedding, and provisions. My extra eighty pounds made little difference to her, but goll-ee, how I had to spraddle out my legs to get my seat down on her broad back!

The three-mile trip up the canyon to where we started the long, steep climb to the top of the Main Range, which forms the east boundary of the Pecos high country, was uneventful. Not so from there on. There were but few signs of a trail, and the stiff, winding climb through aspen thickets, over crisscrossed logs in old burns and windfalls, and, at last, through the dense alpine forests gave us no end of difficulties.

It was "Whoa, Frances, back up, you can't go between those two trees," or "Hold on, Elliott, she'll have to jump that log," and "Look out for that snag, the pack will get torn again," then "Duck or you'll get dragged off by those limbs." But what if the pack did get torn and I got my face scratched by low limbs, or even fell off when the big mare jumped a log? That didn't matter at all, I was going along into a big new world, about which I had heard George Beatty and others spin some wonderful tales.

The tedious three-hour climb up the rugged mountain with her heavy load made old Frances perspire until she was soppy wet all over. Riding behind the pack, I wasn't sweating but, certainly, was being sweat on. My seat and thighs were as wet and salty as if I had sat down in a tub of brine. It wasn't comfortable but it was better than walking and I didn't mind; I was going along, wasn't I?

At last, near noon, we reached the crest of Spring Mountain, a prominent place on the Main Range, at an elevation of about 11,500 feet. We stopped for lunch and to rest the horses a while just below the crest, at the little ice cold spring from which the mountain gets its name. When I got off, I tried to keep my sweat-soaked backside from being noticed but didn't succeed. Mr. Ground said, so that everybody could hear, "What's the matter Elyit, looks like you wet your pants," and everybody laughed but me. Thus reminded, I decided right then I had better run on up the hill out of sight and take prompt action to prevent doing what Mr. Ground had suggested I had already done.

I was reluctant to come back to the crowd right away to be teased, so to kill time I wandered on up the slope to the highest point of Spring Mountain and into the edge of the long opening that lies along its crest. From there the magnificent upper Pecos basin and the majestic high peaks and long ridges in the shape of a huge horseshoe surrounding it came into view.

I stopped, glued to the ground, and stood gazing with unbelieving amazement into what, for me, was a new and wonderful world—the Pecos high country. From then to now it has been an intimate part of my life.

My vocabulary is wholly inadequate to describe the fascinating panorama which burst into sight, or the lasting impression it made upon me. Far across the deep canyons and intervening ridges to the northwest, the triple pinnacles of the rugged Truchas Peaks reared their gray majestic heads almost to the black belly of the frothy, white-topped thunder clouds forming above them. In the crevices and deep gorges, between timber line and their 13,000-foot summits, great drifts of winter's snow lingered on, glistening defiantly in the warm June sun. A little to the east of Truchas Peaks, big, round-topped Cerro Chi-mayosos stood out boldly, but not so high nor so jagged as its neighboring peaks to the west. East of that was Santa Barbara Baldy and the long timber-line ridges on each end of it, forming the watershed divide between the Pecos River and the Santa Barbara, which flows westward into the Rio Grande.

The Main Range, atop which I stood, extended many miles to the north at a fairly even elevation, to join the timber-line divide at the head of the Rio de la Casa. To the south, the Main Range could be seen as far as Elk Mountain, which just touches timber-line about seven miles away. This range breaks off precipitously on the east and was characterized by a very heavily timbered crest except for some unique strips of loggy old burns draped across it. "I'll bet there are grizzly bear in there," I said to myself, not knowing that many years later this very spot would turn out to be one of the most successful bear-hunting camps I ever had.

Turning my gaze back across the beautiful Pecos high country, I saw, directly west, lofty Santa Fe Baldy majestically dominating the dark, dense forests below it. Between Santa Fe Baldy and granite-strewn Truchas Peaks, double-topped Pecos Baldy stood out boldly, with its cliffy east face glistening in the bright sun. Further southward, Lake Peak was poking its little barren top up through vast bluish-purple forests. Still farther on, Glorieta Baldy, which forms the southern end of the west rim of the upper Pecos basin, could be seen but it was not as spectacular as the higher rugged peaks to the north. The wild beauty of the canyons and intervening ridges was little less impressive than the splendid ranges and spectacular peaks and pinnacles forming the horseshoe-shaped basin's rim. In fact, the whole landscape, composed of varying colors and shapes of alpine forests, aspen groves, old burns, and grassy mountain parks, comprised a huge mosaic pattern of wondrous pristine beauty.

In the center of the basin and directly in line with me and the towering Truchas Peaks, lay the five-mile-long, open, grass-topped Hamilton Mesa, framed in deep-green aspen and coniferous forests. This long, prominent central ridge forms the divide between the main Pecos and Mora rivers.

Below and in front of double-peaked, shimmering Pecos Baldy, Round Mountain stood out attractively, its round crest clothed in a blue-green jacket of spruce and fir, with a flaring, grass-patched aspen skirt below.

Beneath the gray cliffs and great rock slides of Truchas Peaks, sprawled the biggest and most formidable forest unit of all. Here, in the midst of the untamed forest, springs and marshes in profusion form the headwaters of the Rio Chi-mayosos, which, in reality, is the left fork of the Pecos River. It required little effort for a ten-year-old boy to imagine that to be real grizzly bear country, also. Just south of the Chimayosos basin, below a long open hogback, whose east face was marked by remarkably uniform horizontal strata of limestone, lay the charming Rito Azul. True to its name, its forests, surrounding a long mountain park, were the bluest in all the area.

Perhaps the most fascinating spot of all the many intriguing features of the interior basin, that caught my eye, was the head of Cebadilloso Canyon. This small but noisy tumbling creek enters the left fork of the Pecos just above Beatty's Cabin, while its source lies against the almost perpendicular slope of the timber-line ridge northeast of Pecos Baldy. A dense, almost impenetrable, alpine forest blankets the entire length of the south side of the canyon. The lower half of the north side of the canyon is covered with fine aspen woods interspersed with clumps of spruce and fir. The upper half opens out into a big and very steep, forest-rimmed, grass-covered slope shaped like a shepherd's staff. The head of the canyon is a veritable amphitheater, with a triangular shaped plot of timber in the center simulating an audience.

As I stood gazing wide eyed at this alluring scene, I could not foresee that, years later, after elk had been restored to the Pecos high country, I would enjoy hunting them there, and have the luck to bag four nice bulls right there over a period of ten years, or that, as this story is being written fifty-six years later, I would choose that very spot to go deer hunting with my son and kill a fine fat mule deer buck right in the amphitheater.

Naturally, I did not know the names of any of these peaks and canyons, except possibly, the Truchas Peaks, but the fact that, to me, they were nameless detracted not at all from their fascinating beauty and splendor. I had heard of Beatty's Cabin and wondered where, in that labyrinth of canyons and ridges, it was located.

All but the first three years of my life had been spent on our little mountain ranch, with little opportunity to see anything of the outside world. Of course, I had been out to Las Vegas, our trading point twenty-five miles away, many times but that trip took one only out of the mountains onto the plains to a town where there were lots of people, and what was there to that? Here, truly, a new world, in all its untamed scenic beauty, lay before me.

I do not know how long I had stood entranced gazing at this wondrous scene when I was brought back to reality and consciousness of a wet crotch and horse-sweat-stained overalls by someone loudly calling, "Elliott, you better come on back and eat your lunch."

The trip down the big mountain to camp, on the Mora River, was just about as tedious as the climb up had been. The caravan went across the broad crest of Spring Mountain north of the high point and through a mile and a half of thickly growing spruce and fir timber to Los Esteros, a big, round marsh in the edge of an extremely loggy old burn. There the maze of crisscrossed logs offered a formidable barrier to further progress. Finally, some faint blazes marking the Harvey Ranch-Beatty's Cabin route were found, and by winding and weaving first this way, then that, we got through, but not without torn packs and skinned horse legs.

Through the aspen bench lands below, we fared better. Down the ridge north of Los Esteros Creek for the last leg of the journey the timber was more open but the route very steep. All of us walked and led our horses, to the relief of both horses and riders. Camp was made at last, a little before sundown, on a flat place where Rito de Los Esteros enters the Mora River, principal tributary of the Pecos.

As soon as the horses were unsaddled and hobbled out to graze in the lush, flower-spangled meadow, some of the folks set about getting the camp in order, making down beds, getting in firewood, etc., while others went fishing. We had brought along snelled hooks and lines and, perhaps, some flies but we didn't have any fishing rods and creels in those days. Instead, a long slender willow pole cut on the ground, a creel improvised out of a burlap bag, or just a forked stick stringer had to suffice. My first assigned job was to catch grasshoppers, of which there was a bountiful supply, for the others to use for bait.

The black-spotted, red-bellied cutthroat trout were biting fast and furiously enough to delight the most ardent disciple of Izaak Walton. It didn't take long to get a big mess for supper, and what a feast we had! Fresh mountain trout rolled in corn-meal, salted, and fried crisp in plenty of bacon grease over a campfire just can't be beat any time, but on this occasion our appetites were so whetted by the arduous trip that the repast was doubly enjoyable and satisfying.

The trip, the feast, and the warm campfire's glow soon made us drowsy and we were ready for beds which had been made down under the big trees on improvised mattresses of carefully placed tips cut from spruce and fir boughs.

Next day everybody fished, some downstream, some up just above camp, and some went away up the Mora and Valdez creeks, above their junction a mile above camp. It was on this trip, I think, that just below camp, in an old heap of driftwood and silt, on Los Esteros Creek, my brother Charlie found and dug out the old skull and antlers of a huge bull elk. The antlers were rather crumbly and there was no telling how long they had been buried there. Elk were supposed to have become extinct in the region in about 1885. Here we had mute evidence that these majestic animals had for certain once roamed this mountain fastness.

The second day, Pa and Mr. Ground determined to ride over to the main Pecos to see how fishing was there. I, of course, begged to go along and, to my delight, I was again, though reluctantly, permitted to do so. More reluctantly was I permitted to ride John, Charlie's pet saddle horse. His stirrups, of course, were away too long so I put my feet in the stirrup straps.

We went up through the Mora Flats to the mouth of the Valdez Creek, then up it a couple of miles through a rough, timbered canyon. At one of the many creek crossings, we saw in the mud a huge, fresh bear track. It looked as big as an elephant track to me, and it was supposed to be a grizzly, but I hadn't yet learned how to tell a grizzly's track from a black bear's track by the long claw marks and its different shape.

Finally, the canyon opened out into less steep aspen- and grass-covered slopes and benches, and we climbed out, crossing the top through a saddle at the northeast end of Hamilton Mesa. We dropped off the ridge heading for the junction of the Pecos River and Rito Padre, its main left fork. There was not much sign of a trail but we found a few tree blazes, probably made by George Beatty going from Harvey's Ranch to his cabin. The last few hundred yards were so steep that we walked and led our horses, hitting the stream just above Beatty's Cabin. We then rode down to the old cabin, stopped and inspected it, and then went on down below the forks of the Pecos and Rito del Padre, where we tied the horses, cut willow poles, and went fishing.

Beatty's Cabin, situated on the little grassy point between the forks of the river, evidently had been abandoned for some time and was in a bad state of repair. The dirt roof was caving in and the chinking was falling out of the log walls. The fireplace, back in the corner, had been appropriated by pack rats for a den, and was filled with a great pile of chips and debris of all kinds, which these industrious little animals, sometimes called trade rats, had collected. The puncheon floor was rotting and the hewn-pole door had fallen from its hinges.

Below the cabin, near the creek, was a prospect hole dug into the side of the mountain, on a vein of reddish quartz walled by mica schist formation. Examining some of the rock, Pa said, "Don't look like much mineral there." Evidently, the old prospector, George Beatty, owner of the "sure good bear knives" and spinner of tall tales, had come to the same conclusion years before and forever abandoned his claim and cabin.

The trout here were bigger but not so plentiful as in the Mora, and after catching a nice mess of the red bellied, black-spotted beauties, we set out for camp. We took a different route out of the canyon, leaving it nearly a mile below the forks, and climbed out over the top of Hamilton Mesa, then went down a dim trail to the junction of the Mora and Valdez, arriving at camp just at dusk. With a lot more fish than we could use in camp, we were ready to go home.

I was happy. I had been on high places and seen a new world. I had penetrated deep into the Pecos high country all the way to Beatty's Cabin. I was now eager to go back home to tell Mother and the younger kids of my adventures. But when we broke camp I made one resolution. I resolved to come back to the gorgeous, fascinating Pecos high country often. That resolution I have faithfully kept, even unto this day.

3
pecos grizzlies

Adventure-packed tales of the prominent and exciting roles played by grizzly bear on the Western frontier are told in both history and legend. The Pecos high country is no exception. That Redmen hunted the area long before Palefaces took over is evidenced by the spearheads and arrow points which may still be found; and there were grizzlies a-plenty until we white men wiped them out. While a fossilized grizzly carcass with an arrow point embedded in the bones has yet to be found, there can be little doubt that, on occasion, the more adventuresome and daring braves tangled with fierce old *ursus horribilis* in mortal combat. The pity is that details of how the attacks were made and the outcome must be left to imagination.

George Beatty spun some wild, hair-raising tales of adventures with grizzlies in the vicinity of his cabin in the 1870's. But a far more authentic early-day account comes to us from the diaries of Professor L. L. Dyche. In June, 1882, Dyche and his student companion, Brown by name, were camped in the upper Pecos wilderness at his "Bear Trail" camp on Rito Del Oso, some six miles southeast of Beatty's Cabin. They had come after specimens of deer, elk, and other mammals, but especially after bear—big grizzly bear.

The very first morning they discovered a well-worn, freshly-used bear trail near their camp, affording unmistakable proof that they were in the right country. Day after day, carrying his heavy Sharp's rifle, Dyche followed fresh grizzly tracks all over the mountains but never could get so much as a glimpse of his fast-traveling, elusive quarry. Discouraged by his strenuous but fruitless efforts, he finally killed a deer for bait and built a scaffold in a nearby tree from which he watched night after night, but foxes and bobcats were the only animals to visit the bait. It is of great interest to note that Dyche made no reference at all to coyotes, which, in later years, became abundant in the area.

Then early one morning, numbed and stiff from spending an unusually chilly night on his precarious perch in the tree, he left it and went to camp to thaw out and get some breakfast. Imagine his utter chagrin and frustration upon returning to the spot a short while later to find that a huge grizzly had come to the deer carcass right after he left, eaten most of it, and gone on before he got back. Enraged, he set out with determination and haste on the monstrous beast's trail and followed it as fast as he could until two o'clock but was unable to catch up. His discouragement bordered on despondency as he wearily dragged himself back to camp.

After a complete rest of two nights and a day, the world looked brighter and he set out again with new determination to find bear—and find them he did, more than he had bargained for. For that story we quote Dyche's own words as recorded by Edwords.

"I got the fox traps at the bait and, as I was looking around, I saw a large bear trail that was very fresh. The bears had been here, there and everywhere. The ground was torn up as if a drove of hogs had been rooting and overturning the logs and stones. There must have been a herd of them, for paths led through the woods in a dozen different directions. I soon found the main trail which was as easy to follow as if a herd of cattle had been along there. I went through a number of grassy parks, down a small stream, up another, and then over a mountain. I followed as rapidly as possible, expecting every minute to see them. They spread destruction in their path. Logs, stumps and stones were turned over and ant hills torn to pieces. I determined to get back to camp and start tomorrow with five days' rations in my haversack, and find those bears or die in the attempt.

"I wandered along revolving my plans in my mind, and came out of the woods on a mesa about two hundred yards wide, flanked on one side by a heavy forest while on the other side was a sheer fall of several hundred feet. I was walking slowly along, looking now and then toward the woods, but not thinking of seeing anything, when suddenly there appeared at the edge of the timber a number of moving objects. As they appeared to be coming toward me, I waited and soon got another glimpse of them about three hundred yards away. They were among the trees, and the sun through the leaves gave them a spotted appearance which convinced me they were goats, for many of the Mexican goats, which are sometimes driven up from Pecos to graze in the area, are spotted. Suddenly there came out of the forest, directly to the west of me and not over seventy yards away, a huge grizzly bear.

"Before I could realize what had happened, out came another, then a third, then a fourth, a fifth, a sixth and a seventh. Just think of it, seven big bears in sight all at once! I think there were four more which I saw, making eleven in all in that band. I knew I was in a desperate situation. On one hand was a bottomless precipice and on the other a herd of the most ferocious animals that roam the mountains. How the sweat did roll off my face! There was only one thing to do and I did it to perfection. I stood perfectly still and let those bears go about their business. They went swinging along in a sort of shambling trot or canter almost as fast as the gait of a horse. I no longer wondered at my not being able to overtake them. Some would stop for a second at a time, turning over logs and stones and then hurry on to overtake the band which moved right along. I was hunting bears but not these bears!

"As soon as they were out of sight in the woods, I hastened to assure myself that I was still alive and wiped the sweat from my face. I could easily have put a bullet through any one of them but what would have happened then? I might have been set upon by the whole gang and would not have made a fair meal for any one of them. I made haste to get into the woods and tried to head them off. I wanted to get a shot at them where I could get shelter in the trees if they attacked me. They unintentionally outwitted me, however, and went up a ridge while I was watching a stream."

After relating the amazing story of his unusual adventure to Brown, his camp companion, Brown suggested that if they were to get a grizzly at all, he had best go back over the long, dim trail to Harvey's Ranch and from there to Las Vegas and get a big bear trap. Dyche didn't like the idea of having to trap a grizzly but, since he had been hounded by such abominable luck, and they were about out of provisions anyway, he reluctantly agreed. So, early the next morning, Brown set out on his mission and left Dyche alone in the wild high country.

Nine days later Brown returned, burros loaded with provisions and a forty-two-pound No. 6 bear trap dangling from Old Reuben's pack saddle. Dyche hastily prepared a supper of hot coffee, biscuits, and broiled steak, and Brown went ravenously to work on them. Again let's take Clarence E. Edwords' version of the incidents that followed:

"This venison is mighty tough," he remarked. "It must have been one of the oldest bucks in the mountains."

"Take another piece," said Dyche.

"It will be better after we've had it a week or two," was Brown's comment, and he took an extra tough bite. "What kind of meat is this, anyhow? It's the toughest venison I ever tasted."

"Maybe it's fox."

"Fox nothing. It's more like burro meat, I should say. I didn't leave any of the jacks here when I went away, did I?"

"It's bear meat, man. A regular old grizzly at that."

"What? Got a bear! Well, if this is a piece of him it must have been the one old Noah had in the ark. Well, I'm glad he didn't get you. Where's the skin? How did you get him?"

"The day you left camp I started out to look at that big trail where my herd went along. I thought there might be some satisfaction in looking at the track if I couldn't see the bears. The trail was a day old, but I followed along without exactly knowing why. After following it for miles I started back to camp, and reached a grassy slope on the side of the mountain and sat down to rest in the edge of it. There was a willow patch in front, and to the east of me and across from the willows was an almost impenetrable forest of spruce trees. Flowing through an opening in this forest was a little stream which joined another rivulet flowing from the willows. As I sat on a log looking across this stream at the spruce forest, I saw something moving among the trees, and from the glimpse I got of it among the spruce branches, I thought it was a deer. I watched very carefully, expecting to see a big mule buck step out into the opening.

"To my great astonishment a huge grizzly bear stepped from the forest at the opening made by the little stream. What a monster he was! He must have been as big as a cow. The wind was in his favor and, getting scent of me; he placed his front feet on a log and began sniffing the air. I could see his big head going up and down, and must confess that I felt a little chill run over me. The old Sharp's rifle always seemed so big and heavy before, but now I wished it was a cannon. I took the best aim possible, holding my breath to prevent muscular movement, and remembering the advice of my father to always see that the sights were on the gun before pulling trigger, and then I fired. The gun belched forth its load with a roar which was echoed by another roar from the bear.

"Here he came growling, rolling, tumbling, falling, jumping, and bellowing, making a terrific noise. I slipped off my shoes, reloaded the gun, placed a handful of cartridges in the crown of my hat by my side, and waited. I thought the whole gang might appear and wanted to be ready for any emergency. The old fellow came on towards me, and I determined that if he ever crossed that stream I would give him another 520-grain bullet. He would get tangled up in a fallen spruce tree and would tear himself loose in a most wonderful manner. He now was in the willows, rolling and tumbling and biting everything that was in his way.

"His strength and activity were simply wonderful. One blow of his mighty paw would have killed the greatest prize-fighter that ever lived. I have heard stories of men killing grizzly bears with their knives, but I don't think it possible for twenty men to have stood before that bear in his death agony. I could now see him very plainly, and could see that he was covered with blood and was getting weaker and weaker every minute as he came on towards me. Just as he reached the edge of the water he spread himself out on all-fours, and there continued throwing up his head, uttering most horrible groans and guttural grunts, while I sat cold and spell-bound under the great excitement. At last he died, seventeen minutes after he had received a ball which would have been instant death to an ox. Then I got up and, went over to where he lay.

"He was a monster indeed. Not fat but so muscular. Streams of blood were running from his mouth where he had broken his great teeth in his death agony. I was under intense excitement, but I noticed his legs were black while his sides and back were of a tawny tint. His tail was very short, so short, in fact, that he could not even sit down upon it.

"It had been raining all day, but I never noticed it as I sat on the log watching the dying throes of the bear. I must confess that I had a pang of remorse as I looked down at the dead monster. I had at last outwitted one of the giants of the forest, but in his death, I had seen the qualities of a big warrior. After finishing my examination of the big fellow I turned about and went to camp, leaving him just where he had fallen. I reached the camp at dark, and would have given a good deal if you had been here to share the enthusiasm with me.

"There was no sleep for me that night. I went over that fearful struggle again and again, and when I dozed off I would wake with a start from a frightful dream of the bear. Next morning I was rested but not refreshed, and after a hurried breakfast I hastened down the canyon where I had left the dead bear. It seemed at times as if it might all be a dream—but no, when I got to the spot there he lay, just as I had left him the night before, dead and cold. Having spent about two hours in taking seventy measurements for future reference, I skinned him. I found that the old fellow had been shot before, for there were two bullets about the size of a forty-four Winchester imbedded in his body, one in his hip and the other in the shoulder. My ball hit him fairly in the neck, cutting the jugular vein and passed entirely through the body, coming out about six inches from the tail near the spine.

"I was almost worn out, but I carried the meat, skin, and head to the big snowdrift and buried them, and dragged myself to camp, where I ate a light supper and then rolled up in my blankets and slept until dawn next morning."

Another monstrous grizzly was taken some weeks later by means of the trap which Brown had packed up the mountain. So Professor Dyche was able to take back two fine specimens of the New Mexico grizzly for the University of Kansas Museum. Many specimens of small mammals, and mule and white-tailed deer also were obtained, but it was a great disappointment that, while he heard of elk in the area, no elk were found.

KICK ME

It was in the late fall of 1897 that a hunting party, consisting of my older brother, Charlie, my brother-in-law, Elwyn Blake, Mr. Hunsaker, Mr. Hemler, and Mr. Rickerman, all from Las Vegas, were camped away up on the Mora fork of the Pecos near its source. There was little snow, but there in the high country cold freezing weather had already set in. Charlie killed a little white-tailed buck the first morning, which provided them with tender camp meat. He also caught a big mess of trout, with improvised grab hooks, through a hole in the ice, out of a deep, mud-bottomed pool, where great numbers had congregated to spend the long winter. Then Elwyn, plagued by a sudden attack of buck fever, emptied his Winchester repeating rifle at a herd of mule deer but failed to draw blood.

Everywhere in the many marshy spots in the area they found sign where bear had been rooting and overturning the sod, in search of tender roots and bulbs. It was evident that there had been plenty of bear, big grizzly bear, there, but the sign was all old and the party concluded that the bitter cold nights had driven them into hibernation.

Mr. Rickerman was extremely eager to kill a grizzly, and hoped to find at least one that had not yet gone into his winter den, or, perhaps he could find a den. On the morning of the last day he gazed hard at an old, foot-long grizzly track frozen in the mud and said, "I'd give a hundred dollars for a shot at the old boy that made that track." Then he set out alone to make one last desperate effort to find a bear.

Late that afternoon a shot from his .40-82 Winchester boomed and echoed in the canyon below camp. "Rick's got his bear sure as shootin'. Let's make him pay off when he comes in," Elwyn said.

Pretty soon Rickerman rushed into camp all out of breath and trembling with excitement. "Kick me! Kick me!" he shouted.

"What's the matter, what's wrong, didn't you get him?"

"Kick me! Just kick me!" the overwrought hunter repeated again and again. So Elwyn kicked his backside two or three times, but good and hard. Then they got his sad story.

"I saw that big old bear awfully busy rooting around in a marsh like a hog," he said, "but it was too far to shoot. So I got down on my hands and knees and crawled up the canyon for two hundred yards, keeping out of sight as best I could. At last I peeped over a log and there he was, not a hundred yards away. He looked as big as a bull. I was shaking like an aspen leaf so I rested my gun on the log and drew bead for his heart. At last I had my grizzly where I wanted him. When I pulled the trigger I didn't see how I could miss. But damn it, I did, and he was out of sight in a hurry. I'll never get another chance. Somebody kick me again!"

MORE ABOUT GRIZZLIES

Right after the turn of the century, two fine men, with deep-seated love of the mountains and forests in their hearts, left their homes in Arkansas and settled in Las Vegas, New Mexico. They were C. W. and Frank J. Wesner. Jeff Keene, a neighbor of ours, took them on their first trip into the upper. Pecos Mountains with a string of pack burros. They promptly fell in love with the beauty and majesty of the towering peaks, deep blue-green forests, and talking waters. They went back many times and it was my pleasure to pack them in more than once, the last time in 1908.

Grizzly bear never were taken easily. There were no packs of dogs in that country that could be counted upon to stop a grizzly. The chances of getting a shot by still hunting or trailing one up were pretty slim. Nevertheless, hunters regularly wore themselves out trying. When all other methods failed they often would resort to the use of traps, a method of taking bear considered unsportsmanlike, and prohibited by law today.

Early in August, 1906, a party of six, with Frank Wesner as the kingpin, packed in to Beatty's Cabin, determined to get a-big grizzly bear. They took tents and other equipment necessary to set up a comfortable camp, and a big supply of provisions, as well as two bear traps. In addition to the pack burros, they took an extra along to kill for bear bait. The very first night, Frank got bit on the ear by a pack rat and was terribly scared, thinking it was a poisonous snake, but he suffered no ill effects. Trout fishing was excellent, young grouse were plentiful, and in their comfortable camp the young men lived and dined like kings. They found some good bear sign away up near the head of the Chimayosos, near Truchas Peaks. They hunted diligently, but without success. It was like hunting a needle in a haystack trying to find a lone grizzly in that vast expanse of forest. So they killed a burro for bait to attract the bear. From here on, we will let Frank tell the story in his own words. He says:

"After visiting the carcass several times, we, at last, found the big bear had come to feed on it. We built a V-shaped pen around the burro carcass and set two big steel traps in the entrance, feeling sure we would have our bear next morning. Full of anticipation, we cautiously approached the set to find that Mr. Bruin had been there, torn the pen down, and dragged the carcass out the back way and there eaten his fill, missing the traps entirely.

"There was a large spruce log near where the burro carcass had been left so I decided to build a pen that could not be wrecked so easily. We moved the carcass up close to the big log, which was held up off the ground a foot or more by limbs, making its top four feet off the ground. We then built a long wing of heavy aspen logs at a slight angle to the big log, thinking that the bear would have to walk between the big log and the wing fence to get to the carcass. We set one trap at the entrance and the other near the carcass, confident the bear would put one of his big feet in the trap when he came back for his supper.

"We didn't rightly foresee the astuteness of this wise old fellow. Next morning we found he had been back all right but had outsmarted us again. Instead of going in to the bait the easy way he had climbed upon the big high log and, in some way, reached down and pulled the carcass up over the log and just about finished it. No bear again, and our previous high hopes fell pretty low. We better get on the ball for there wasn't much burro meat left.

"We gathered up what was left of the hide and bones, put them back between the log and the wing fence, and staked the hide down good and solid with some big, dead tree limbs, so he would have to do some real pulling to move it at all. This looked like our last chance.

"Next morning, long before we got to the spot, we heard excited bellowing of cattle, as if something unusual was happening. We rushed on up there, and the cattle ran away as we approached. We were sure something had happened. Did we have the big old bear or had we caught a cow? A bear, when freshly caught, bawls and bellows like a bull in distress and might naturally attract a bunch of cattle. We hoped that was it.

"The ground was all torn up and from the aspen thicket below we heard the clanking of traps and chains, and soon a glimpse of the raging beast confirmed our highest hopes. We had our big old grizzly bear. His head was covered with froth and he was the maddest animal I ever saw. He would rush at us as far as the trap chains would let him, hair all bristled up and popping his teeth viciously. He had stepped in the trap nearest the bait with one front foot, and, in backing out, had stepped in the other with the opposite hind foot, so we had the wise old fellow cross hobbled.

"As we watched his frantic efforts to break loose and get at us we kept him well covered with our high-powered rifles. But the trap toggles had become tangled solidly in the thicket and he couldn't get loose. One of the party, Henry Brown, from California, had a .22 caliber Stevens target rifle which he used to kill grouse. Jokingly, I said, 'Henry, think you can kill him with your .22'? Whereupon Henry, taking me at my word, pulled up and shot that huge grizzly right below the ear and, to our utter, unbelieving amazement, he dropped like a pig, stone dead! He was a magnificent specimen and I'll bet the only big grizzly ever killed with a little old .22 rifle.

"That was on September 6, 1906, and we had been in camp for a month. We were out of provisions but loath to leave this thrill-packed wilderness paradise to go home. So Henry and I rode over to Mora, a long day's ride each way, and got a big supply of provisions and we stayed on through the enchanting month of September, feasting on grouse and cutthroat trout, enjoying to the utmost our camp at Beatty's Cabin. Incidentally, we tried eating some of the old grizzly bear meat, but no matter how we cooked it, or for how long, boiled, fried, broiled, or roasted, the longer we chewed on a piece of it the bigger it got."

The very next year, Frank Wesner had another exciting experience with a grizzly, but with a less gratifying outcome. But let's permit Frank to tell it in his own words. He says:

"In August 1907, I rounded up four or five young fellows for companions and we packed out from Las Vegas, going up by the Barker Ranch on Sapello Creek, and camped on top of Spring Mountain. We killed a burro for bear bait, and did some scouting for sign while we were waiting for the burro carcass to get ripe so that bear would find it. We waited a few days but didn't see much sign, and, as nothing visited the bait, we decided that the next morning we would move camp to higher country.

"The next morning when we went to look for our horses and burros they were gone. We set out afoot to look for them, but they seemed to have scattered in all directions. We found some tracks headed south toward the trail we had come up on, but when we reached the trail the only tracks there were the ones we had made on our trip up. So we diligently searched in other directions and, finally, found our animals in the head of Trampas Creek.

"They were terribly frightened when they saw us, threw up their heads and away they went. Finally, by circling them, we were able first to catch some of the old gentle ones and then the others. We discovered there was one burro missing, and one old white burro, named Noah, had a fresh deep scratch from the top of his head to the end of his nose. We were then quite sure our animals had been raided by either a bear or a lion.

"A couple of days later, while out looking for the missing burro, we saw some ravens flying around and, after watching them awhile, we saw them settle down in a spot about a half a mile away, so we quickly headed in that direction. One of the boys had brought along a bull terrier pup and when we got near the place where the ravens had settled down, the pup started barking and went bounding down over a little rimrock. When we found him he was eating on the remains of our missing animal, and there was plenty of sign that a big grizzly bear had sure enough killed our burro. Who was hunting who anyway?

"We quickly returned to camp and got two bear traps and set them at the carcass, believing we would surely get the big bear. Next morning we were up bright and early fully expecting some thrilling excitement and then some bear steaks for dinner. To our disappointment we found the bear had not been back. We continued to visit the traps for two or three days but when the big burro-killing bear failed to return, we decided it had probably been an old roving grizzly, and moved our camp to the Mora Flats. There we had the best of fishing and spent a delightful two weeks in the mountain paradise."

In June, 1908, my brother Charlie and I chased a big grizzly with two cubs all over the top of Spring Mountain. The old bear turned over rocks, tore up logs, and rooted in the marshy places in search of food, while the playful cubs would lag behind, climb to the top of big, hard snowdrifts, slide down them, and then run to catch up with their mother. We never were able to catch up but often were excitingly close.

Two weeks later, while camped alone at Spring Mountain, I had better luck and killed four grizzlies. But that is another story, to be told some other time, maybe when I compile the story of all my bear-hunting experiences.

4

forestry comes to the pecos high country

It seems the Pecos high country has been enhanced by some unique, extraordinary quality from the beginning. Proof lies in the fact that it has the distinction of being the second oldest of all the national forests in existence today. It was withdrawn, or created, as the Pecos River Forest Reserve by proclamation of President Harrison in 1892. Actually, the Yellowstone Park Timberland Reserve, in 1891, was the first withdrawal. The Pecos River Forest Reserve became a national forest, along with many other reserves created after the Pecos, when the official designation was changed.

While we are accustomed to think of Theodore Roosevelt as the father of the national forests, many major battles had been waged with an obstinate Congress, some lost, some won, and the groundwork laid before Teddy became president, upon the assassination of President McKinley, September 14, 1901. Presidents Harrison, Cleveland, and McKinley were all in favor of preservation and regulated use of the forested and watershed areas of the public domain.

The late Gifford Pinchot, first U. S. forester, said, "In 1891 [Harrison's administration], the most important legislation in the history of forestry in America slipped through Congress without question and without debate. It was an amendment to the Act of March 3, 1891, 'For the Repeal of the Timber and Stone Act and for other Purposes,' and it authorized creation of Forest Reserves. This was the beginning and the basis of our whole National Forest System."

It is worthy of note that the creation of the Pecos Forest Reserve, embracing the Pecos high country, was not long delayed after the authority for creation of forest reserves was given. It is obvious that watershed protection was the primary purpose of the withdrawal; and, indeed, today that outweighs all other considerations, with recreation a close second.

The remarkable circumstance of this act slipping through Congress without question and without debate was due to the fact that Congress had been softened up in the many previous battles spearheaded by that indomitable conservationist, Gifford Pinchot, the American Forestry Association, and other leaders who clearly foresaw the inevitable slow death of a nation unless the prevailing ruthless exploitation and devastation of vital natural resources were halted. Today we are prone to take for granted our great system of national forests embracing a total of 180,000,000 acres. We forget that the invaluable watershed, timber, wildlife, recreation, and grazing resources embraced within their boundaries were preserved for the benefit of the public generally, of the present and future generations, only because foresighted patriotic men, before and around the turn of the century, had the intestinal fortitude and altruistic determination to fight and win the battle against entrenched despoilers and their cohorts—corrupt politicians. The pioneer champions of conservation of vital natural resources fought and lost many battles but won a few crucial ones against great odds. Let's give them a hand! But while we are doing so, let's not drop our guards for one minute. If we are to preserve for regulated multiple use the vast and varied resources of the national forests, it behooves us to be ever watchful and, as Teddy Roosevelt suggested, "Speak softly, but carry a big stick."

When the Pecos River Forest Reserve was created, no provision was made for its administration, management, and use, or the practice of forestry. It received no protection; the area was merely set aside and withdrawn, legally at least, from every form of use. No timber could be cut, no forage grazed, no minerals mined, and, technically, it was illegal for any man to trespass upon it. Actually, not much attention was paid to its status; however, one all important thing was accomplished— the title to the lands was preserved in the government.

This same condition prevailed on all forest reserves throughout the West, created between 1891 and June 4, 1897, and involving about forty million acres. On February 22, 1897, ten days before President Cleveland's term expired, thirteen forest reserves, embracing over seventeen million acres, were added to the twenty-three million acres already withdrawn.

Failure of Congress to provide for legitimate regulated use of the forest reserves, as was desired by Gifford Pinchot and President Harrison, at the time authority was given for their creation was a very grave mistake. That omission, more than anything else, touched off the bitter fight against the reserves which was waged vigorously for years by grazing, timber, and mining interests of the West. It was not until June 4, 1897, that legislation was finally passed, giving the Secretary of the Interior authority to protect and administer the forest reserves and open them to regulated use and the practice of forestry. Another thing that caused misunderstandings and opposition to the forest reserves, and later to national forests, is the name, which, to some, implies a totally-forested area. On the contrary, they are not, and never were, intended to meet that requirement. Watershed protection was, and is, one of the primary purposes of the national forests, yet the land cover is often a veritable mosaic pattern of timber, brush, mountain meadows and parks, aspen thickets, and rock slides. The national forests are manageable only as a unit, and it is a ridiculous proposal to try, as some interests do, to eliminate the non-timbered lands just because they have no merchantable timber on them.

When the forest reserves were put under administration, they were kept in the Department of the Interior; while the Division of Forestry, created in 1880, was in the Department of Agriculture and, hence, had no authority over the forest reserves. Can one imagine anything so ridiculous and inconsistent? Yet, that situation prevailed for seven long years. What was even worse, the Department of the Interior was then steeped in politics and its early administration of the forest reserves was very bad. Supervisors and rangers, in most cases, were incompetent political appointees recommended by congressmen from the Midwest and eastern states, while those appointed directly by the Commissioner of the General Land Office were even worse. Not a few were given appointments for the sake of their health —consumptives unable to perform their duties. This brought the forest reserves into even greater disrepute. But because the theory upon which they were based was entirely sound, they survived later to be managed by the finest organization of the federal government.

As to the Pecos River Forest Reserve, the first forest supervisor was a man by the name of Wilhoyt. He and a ranger, whose name I do not recall, were sent, after passage of the act of June 4, 1897, to take charge of the reserve. They were political appointees from Kentucky and knew nothing of conditions in the West, had no idea how to deal with Western people, and even less knowledge of what their jobs should be or how to do them.

The supervisor and his ranger decided to make an inspection trip into the Pecos high country and employed Tom Stewart, a young Western mountain man, to pack and guide them into Beatty's Cabin country. Stewart later became forest ranger himself, and a good one, too, and afterward was supervisor of the Pecos Forest. It was in July, and the rainy season, characterized by clear mornings with heavy thunder showers by noon almost every day, was on. Tom noted with secret amusement that, instead of the conventional saddle slickers rolled behind their saddles, they each carried an umbrella.

As they followed him up the trail on the somewhat skittish horses which he had rented to them at a dollar a day, Tom kept visualizing what might happen when the umbrellas were opened. Unaccustomed to riding, progress was slow, and by the time they got to Hamilton Mesa, the usual thunder clouds had rolled up, lightning flashed, and it began to rain. Tom donned his slicker, but all the while keeping his eye on the greenhorn government officials with their "bumbershoots."

Supervisor Wilhoyt was first to get his big black umbrella opened up, but that was all new to the Western pony. Frightened out of his wits, the horse went wild, dropped his head and began to pitch high, wide, and handsome. At the very first jump, Wilhoyt lost both stirrups and the bridle reins, but held on tight to the handle of the bobbing umbrella. The second wild jump threw the tenderfoot supervisor higher than a kite. He sailed through the air with the greatest of ease and landed all sprawled out on his back in a snowberry bush still gripping the handle of the umbrella. Tom said that was the funniest thing that he ever saw happen. Without doubt, it is the only recorded parachute landing from the back of a bucking horse. The inspection trip ended then and there, and there is no record that the high-flying supervisor ever did penetrate into the real Pecos high country.

The story is told of another one of those tenderfoot, political rangers, a dud as well as a dude, who put his saddle on the horse backwards. The local cowboys made a big joke out of it and laughed to beat hell. Chagrined, the greenhorn ranger, evidently not without a sense of humor, said, "The joke is on you this time, you just don't know which way I'm going today."

I believe, after Wilhoyt, R. C. McClure was made supervisor of the Pecos River Forest Reserve and, perhaps, the ranger service began to improve some. Tom Stewart, who later became supervisor, was employed first by McClure in May, 1902. Then a man by the name of Langenberg was sent up from the Gila Forest Reserve to replace McClure, but he remained only a short while.

After that, a man named Hanna was put in charge, and, it seems from all reports, he was somewhat more competent than his predecessors. It is reported that he got into trouble for issuing his son a permit for four hundred cattle to be grazed on the Hamilton Mesa. He was ousted in 1903, and R. J. (Bob) Ewing, who, I believe, was a local man, replaced him. Ewing didn't last long, as he got into trouble with an inspector, son-in-law of Binger Hermann, commissioner of the General Land Office.

Supervisor Hanna was then reinstated and, it seems, was awarded eight months' back pay, but died in 1904 without collecting it. One good thing Hanna did during his administration was to retain Tom Stewart as a ranger. That was fortunate because Stewart, although lacking in education, was a good Western man, spoke Spanish as well as English, and knew the local people and how to deal with them. Tom was especially efficient in getting along with the native Spanish-speaking people. He was one of the real pioneer forest rangers, who literally and figuratively blazed many a trail and who made good. He remained with the Service for many years and, despite his educational handicap, finally became supervisor. I met Tom Stewart first right after he went to work as forest ranger in May, 1902, when he came to put out a fire on Sapello Creek, near where we lived. I was later to work as ranger under him as supervisor.

The following description of the general early administration of the forest reserves in the Western states, under the Department of the Interior, is given by Gifford Pinchot. He says:

"Since jobs on the Forest Reserves were for distribution to politicians, Commissioner Binger Hermann of the General Land Office was careful to get his while the getting was good. The average appointee was plenty bad enough, but Binger's personal appointments were horrible."

He had three brothers-in-law on the forest reserve, one described by Pinchot as "an old man absolutely worthless in his position"; another as "ignorant, general report makes him incompetent, and in league with the sheepmen"; a third as "an ideally unfit man, utterly useless in every way."

Mr. Pinchot goes on to say, "Political appointees, many of whom had never even seen a Western Forest, were sent thousands of miles from all over the Union, to handle Western Forest Reserves. . . . The Supervisor in South Dakota, almost purely a politician utterly without experience, came from Indiana. Connecticut furnished to Washington State a perfectly worthless young man. Moreover, in addition to those who were no good whatever, and those who might have been good under good leadership, some were crooks, all together bad eggs."

Thus, we see that, even though the first big hurdle in the program for conservation of our natural resources had been cleared by the passage of an act, in 1891, authorizing the creation of forest reserves and the second by the act of June 4, 1897, placing them under administration and authorizing their use, there was much yet to be done.

Referring to this latter act, Gifford Pinchot said, "The Secretary of the Interior was given charge of the Forest Reserves 'and he may make such rules and regulations and establish such service as will insure the objects of such reservations, namely, to regulate their occupancy and use and to preserve the forests therein from destruction.' This was the milk in the coconut. It made forest protection and forest management possible, and it is still today, over fifty years afterward, the law under which the National Forests are administered, and forestry practiced upon them."

Thus, as is too often the case, good laws were failing because of bad administration. But all the while another battle was on to correct the situation in which so much of the vital resources of the country was at stake. In 1898, the Division of Forestry in the Department of Agriculture was in trouble. Let us remember that the forest reserves were under the administration of the Department of the Interior. Dr. Bernard E. Fernow, head of the little Forestry Division since 1886, resigned to head up the newly-established forest school at Cornell University. Secretary of Agriculture James Wilson offered the position to Gifford Pinchot. Reluctantly he considered it, then, later, eagerly accepted it. That was the very best thing that could have happened, even though the Division of Forestry was a microscopic outfit, having only ten people in it, some good and some not so good, as the new chief said.

The Forestry Division, from that day on, had as its primary objective the putting of the practice of forestry into the private and public forests of America. Since it had no jurisdiction over the public forest reserves, it had to attack the problem first in private forests, where, under Pinchot's leadership, it soon established itself and proved its worth. With this new prestige, the division, backed by both the President and the Secretary of Agriculture, started a campaign to get the forest reserves transferred to the Department of Agriculture, where they belonged. In July, 1901, the little, but growing, division was promoted to the Bureau of Forestry, with a membership of 179. Along about that time, the Department of the Interior began placing upon it demands for forestry management advice, forest working plans, etc. You may be sure Forester Pinchot and his associates lost no opportunity to inject sound ideas and competent personnel, wherever possible, into the federal forest reserve administration.

But there was little satisfaction in making plans for others to carry out or not, as they chose, or to be haphazardly carried out by politically-appointed administrative personnel. So it was that the contest to get the forest reserves turned over to the Department of Agriculture, to be administered by the Bureau of Forestry, grew hotter with each session of Congress. While President McKinley favored this move, a more potent booster came when Theodore Roosevelt was elevated to the Presidency.

Even with the strongest kind of backing, the transfer was blocked by Congress in one way or another, until February 1, 1905. The successful effort was the result of an American Forestry Congress, January 2 to 6, 1905, called by the American Forestry Association. So great was public pressure developed by the carefully laid plans of this forestry congress, that H. R. 8460, the Transfer Act, passed both houses of Congress easily and was eagerly signed by President Roosevelt, on February 1, the same day it reached him. The seven-year battle had been won, and the President's contribution toward bringing about the new regime was very great indeed. As a matter of fact, President Theodore Roosevelt, undoubtedly, made the greatest contribution to conservation of natural resources of any man who ever lived. During his administration, 1902 to 1909, the area within forest reserve boundaries increased from 62,354,965 acres to 194,505,325 acres. He vigorously backed the administration, development, and management of the forest reserves on the basis of the greatest good for the greatest number for the longest time.

The forest reserves were soon to be renamed "national forests" as we know them today, and by a provision of the Appropriation Act of March 3, 1905, the Bureau of Forestry became the Forest Service. We again quote from Pinchot, commenting on the new status of the old forest service: "We [now] had the power as we had the duty, to protect the Reserves for the use of the people, and that meant stepping on the toes of the biggest interests of the West. From that time on, it was fight, fight, fight. We who took over the Forest Reserves preferred the small man before the big man because his need was greater. . . . The Forest Service was the first government organization not only to assert that the small man had the first right to the natural resources of the West, but actually to make it stick. Better help a poor man make a living for his family than help a rich man get richer still. That was our battle cry and our rule of life. It was true and it was right and no one could openly attack it. And that was one more reason why it aroused the big men to fury. Because of it, came most of the really dangerous opposition to the Service and the National Forests."

On that foundation, Forester Gifford Pinchot, assisted by his zealous and worthy associates, Overton W. Price, the organizer; George W. Woodruff, law officer; Henry Solon Graves, forester and executive; Albert F. Potter, grazier, recruited from the Arizona Woolgrowers' Association; Herbert W. Smith, publicity director; and others, built the foundation and framework of what is today generally recognized as the best department of the federal government—the U. S. Forest Service. The Pecos River Forest Reserve and later National Forest was, at all times, a unit of the big, over-all forestry program.

About the time of the transfer of the forest reserves to the Department of Agriculture, L. F. Kneipp came up from Arizona to take charge of the Pecos and to straighten out some troubles which had developed. He was the first really well-qualified man to hold that position and he got things off, at last, to a pretty good start. His rangers were local men: Tom Stewart, at Cleveland; Lee Williams, at Glorieta; L. H. Mosiman, at Beulah; and Reynolds, at Truchas. Mr. Kneipp's stay on the Pecos was short but he served long and well with the Forest Service, in various capacities, and is now retired and living in Washington, D. C.

Shortly after the transfer to the Department of Agriculture was made, a lot of cloth posters were put up over the forests in order to bring about a better understanding with the people, advising them of their rights, limitation of use, and the status of the lands, and warning against forest fires, illegal cutting of timber, etc. The notices were printed and signed with the name of James Wilson, Secretary of Agriculture. A ranger was tacking up one of these posters when a young Spanish-American, who had had only limited educational advantages, came along. Laboriously, he read through the whole text out loud, while the ranger stood by ready to answer any questions he might ask. Finally, he came to the signature, puzzled over it a while, then said, "Jee-ma-see Weelson, say-cray-ta-ray, a-gree-cool-too-ray; you Jees-ma-see Weelson?" The ranger was duly appreciative of the compliment.

After Kneipp, the next Forest Supervisor was Ross McMillan, a man of considerable ability and a pretty good administrator. He not only had charge of the Pecos National Forest but the Jemez and Carson Forests, as well, and Tom Stewart was his deputy. It was under Ross McMillan that

I took the Civil Service examination for forest ranger on April 23 and 24, 1908.

The examination consisted of a one-day written test and one-day field test. The field test included marking saw timber for cutting, scaling logs, compass and chain land survey work, riding, and packing. In the riding and packing test, we were each given two horses, a Western style riding saddle, a pack saddle and pair of paniers, and a two-man camp outfit. The camp outfit consisted of two bed rolls, a big tarp, camp cooking utensils and dishes, a week's supply of provisions, and, for fire-fighting tools, a rake, a shovel, and an ax. The saddles and whole outfit were scattered about in disorder. We were required to saddle both horses, gather up and pack the whole camp outfit on one of them, get on the saddle horse and lead the pack horse, then trot the horses for a hundred yards, lope them another hundred and come back in a walk. We were graded on the time it took to pack up ready to start, riding ability, and the neatness and security of the pack upon return—a very good test of skill.

One of the fellows got his pack on in pretty good shape and was ready to start off when he discovered he had forgotten the Dutch oven. Hastily, he tied it to the rear cinch of the pack saddle and started off with it swinging under the horse's belly. The horse allowed as how he wouldn't stand for that and promptly bucked the pack off, scattering bedding, groceries, and tools all over the place. The young would-be ranger did a lot better on his examination the next year, I understood.

Having passed the ranger examination with a grade of 86, I was given a job on the Jemez National Forest on January 1, 1909. I was stationed at Cuba which was, at that time, about the most remote and toughest section of the state. My knowledge of the Spanish language and the traits and habits of the Spanish-American people who constituted 98 per cent of the population of the area, stood me in good with them and I got along without serious trouble. We strictly followed our instructions, however, never to go anywhere, even from house to barn without our side arms.

We issued a lot of free use permits for firewood, house logs, fence posts, poles, etc., to the local people, and had to send a carbon copy in to the supervisor's office. One day I got one back from the office with a note scribbled on it which I couldn't make out, but the initials under it were those of my supervisor, Ross McMillan, and I knew something was wrong. Finally, Winfred Bletcher, another ranger, with whom I was batching, made out what the note said: "Illegible, rewrite and return." We were even and I wanted to keep it that way, so I wrote another note and attached it to the permit and returned it to the supervisor; it said, "I'm awfully sorry, but I just couldn't make out what your note said, so am returning the permit since it is your copy." It was true, I couldn't read it; Bletcher had. No more permits were sent back to me.

In the fall of 1909, the Jemez, Pecos, and Carson Forests were split up. Ross McMillan kept the Carson; Frank E. Andrews came up from a deputy supervisor position on the Gila National Forest to take charge of the Jemez; and Tom Stewart was promoted to supervisor of the Pecos. In the shuffle, at my old friend Tom Stewart's request, I was transferred to the Pecos National Forest and assigned to the district embracing my old stomping ground, the Pecos high country, where I remained for three years. Needless to say, nothing could have made me happier than to be back again in that wonderful country which has always been so dear to me.

After three years as ranger in the magic Pecos high country, I got into some difficulties with the regional forester and was transferred to the Carson National Forest. While I didn't like it at the time, it was the best thing that could have happened to me, for it was my great privilege to serve there for a time under Supervisor Aldo Leopold, who later became an outstanding conservationist and wildlife authority of national prominence. I served on the Carson National Forest as ranger, land examiner, deputy supervisor and forest supervisor until April, 1919, when I resigned to go into the cattle ranching business on a mountain ranch adjacent to the Pecos high country.

Eventually, the Jemez and Pecos Forests were combined to form the Santa Fe National Forest and, today, the two units are designated as the Pecos and Jemez Divisions of the Santa Fe National Forest. But a mere change in names cannot alter the refreshing magnificence of the Pecos high country.

Tom Stewart was succeeded as forest supervisor in 1915 by Don P. Johnston, now president of the American Forestry Association. Then came Joseph C. Kircher, Frank C. Andrews for a long time, Lee Wang, K. D. Florck, and the present incumbent, C. A. Merker, all highly competent and efficient administrators.

5

boys, bear, and trout a-plenty

In the summer of 1903, some neighbor boys and I made a trip to the Pecos high country. We made our camp under a clump of big blue-spruce trees near the junction of the Mora and Valdez creeks, across the Hamilton Mesa ridge from Beatty's Cabin. Although we had no tent, the widespread drooping limbs of the bushy trees kept us dry when it rained.

For our bed, we made a soft, thick mattress of uniformly-placed spruce bough tips. Over this we spread, lengthwise, one end of our six-by-fourteen-foot tarpaulin. Next was a heavy, homemade comfort, then a pair of soft wool blankets to sleep between, another comfort, and then the tarp was doubled back from the foot of the bed over all. Air mattresses and sleeping bags were camp luxuries we had never heard of, but all the same, we had a bed fit to satisfy even a royal devotee of Morpheus.

There were three of us sixteen- and seventeen-year-old boys: Ed Heinlen, Jeff Ground, and I. The three of us had to sleep in one bed, and we drew straws to see who would sleep in the middle, for none of us liked it. This time I was the unlucky one. But after all, just three in a bed was better than five and, in that respect, we were more fortunate than King Solomon who, the Good Book says, slept with his forefathers.

The first afternoon, while trout fishing up the Mora near the mouth of Rito del Oso, we had seen a lot of fresh bear sign which had been made by a grizzly. Rotten logs had been torn to pieces and rocks turned over where the long-clawed old bruin had foraged for grubs, ants, and other insects.

In one place a yellow jackets' nest had been dug out, and in another the big brute had rooted around like a hog, in a marshy place, in search of tender morsels of roots and bulbs. We wished for the big rifle and dogs, which had been left in camp, and when we noted that the big, five-toed track was so fresh that the water was still muddy where he had stepped in a sluggish puddle, we turned back toward camp in a hurry.

That night sleep was slow to come. We lay awake in our soft, warm bed gazing at the blinking stars as they peeked in under the branches of the trees which served as a roof over our heads. We talked for a long time about bear and bear hunting, and were still making fantastic plans for a big bear hunt when, at long last, we fell asleep. Perhaps tomorrow we would go bear hunting instead of fishing.

Just how or where the hunt got started is not quite clear, but it seems the dogs had hit a bear trail and were working it fairly well as we followed on our stout, sure-footed mounts. The huge' track was not old but the scent was faint because it had been dampened down by a light shower of rain about dawn. The dogs worked out the course of the track, as only a good pack can, picking up the faint scent first from the soft, damp earth, then from a rock or a bunch of grass, giving tongue freely whenever a strong whiff of old bruin assailed their nostrils.

Up out of the canyon they climbed, zigzagging back and forth as the woolly monster had varied his course to turn over a rock here and tear up a log there, in search of miniature tidbits of food. Where vegetation was lush on one aspen bench he had grazed on the top's of succulent angelica weed, "osha" as the native New Mexicans call it, an herb of which bear are particularly fond. Here the dogs did a lot of barking and baying, but made little progress in the wet, knee-deep vegetation. In the loose dirt of a gopher hill we saw a clear print of the bear's huge foot for the first time, and were we delighted to see the marks of the long, heavy claws made away out three inches ahead of the toe pads, confirming our fondest hopes that it truly was a big grizzly.

After the pack had laboriously worked the track around the slope into a forest of spruce and fir, which had shed the raindrops and thus left a dry trail beneath the trees, they were off again at a good clip. The dogs now opened up enthusiastically, hounds baying and our two mongrels barking sharply. We touched spurs to our horses and followed on trying our best to keep up. My hat was dragged off by a low limb, but to heck with it, for we had to stay near the pack. We thought the dogs had jumped our quarry but, knowing that a grizzly can't climb a tree as a black bear so easily does.

We were prepared for a long chase before the dogs would be able to bring him to bay.

Suddenly the pack slowed down. Could they have stopped him so soon? "Get your gun out of the scabbard. Don't miss!" But there was no bear there. Instead, the trail led out into one of the worst tangled messes of logs in an old burn that we ever did see. The hounds were finding it almost impossible to work out the trail, which went first under, then over, logs and along them, but finally, persistence and keen noses got the pack through that entanglement and out into the green forest again still hot on the old bear's trail.

If the dogs had trouble in that maze of fallen trees we, even though mounted on excellent mountain horses, had double trouble. In our extreme anxiety and excitement, we forced the horses to jump wide masses of knotty, breast-high logs at the risk of crippling them and ourselves. Miraculously, it seemed, we finally got through all in one piece and without a limping horse.

By then the dogs had gone on far ahead, their trail music reaching us from across the canyon. From the higher pitched tone of their voices and the tremor of excitement in them, we knew for sure this time the old fellow had been jumped. We wondered whether he would run and run as the species usually does or if he would have the temerity to stop and defy the dogs. Would the canine pack have the guts to go in on *Ursus horribilis* from behind and make him back up against a cliff or a log to defend his rear? Would they have good sense and agility enough to grab a bite out of the seat of his pants and get out of the way of his vicious paws and powerful jaws? If we got a shot, would the heavy lead slug from the old .45-70 bring him down?

All these questions raced through our young, inexperienced minds as we rode recklessly, trying to overtake the noisy pack and its formidable quarry. What a chase! What thrills and exhilarating excitement! Never had we been on such a hunt.

A sudden change to almost hysterical, sharp, staccato barking told us the big fellow was at bay, no doubt about it.

"Whoa! Slow down! Get your gun," someone said. Almost instantly we were off, horses tied up, and we were sneaking quietly through the timber to get a shot. All of a sudden we spied the huge, grizzled old bear backed up against a big log fighting the dogs off despite their frenzied efforts to get at him, first from one side and then the other. He looked as big as an elephant and far more vicious.

I raised the rifle, steadied the heavy barrel against a tree, took good aim, and squeezed the trigger. Snap! The cartridge failed to fire. Perhaps in the excitement, I had not loaded the rifle. I pumped the lever hard and fast, throwing another cartridge into the chamber—but, alas, too late! The enormous brute had either heard, smelled, or seen us and had broken and run with the baying pack in hot, noisy pursuit.

Getting back to our horses as quickly as possible, we untied them, jumped on, and followed as fast as we could. We raced through the forests and logs, aspen thickets, and rock slides, uphill and down, in a desperate effort to keep up. Horses were dripping wet with sweat and their sides heaving from the mountain race. Our knees were bruised and our hands and faces scratched and bleeding but we paid no attention to it. What a marvelous chase! We topped the ridge, and then headed hell-bent down toward the main Pecos. For a while it looked as though the old bugger would never stop, but at long last he did, this time against a cliff on the steep, timbered slope overlooking Beatty's Cabin.

Again we were slipping quietly up for a shot, and this time I made certain the heavy rifle was loaded. The tired, panting dogs were baying viciously and worrying Mr. Bruin magnificently. I would have to be careful not to hit a dog. As I got ready to shoot, it seemed suddenly to be getting dark. In the feverish anticipation and excitement of the chase, we had not noticed a big, ominous, black thunder cloud forming right overhead. But there it was, and all of a sudden lightning flashed, the cloud reared up and fell over backwards, and the rain poured out, not in torrents, but in a veritable waterspout. Never before had I seen so much water or gotten drenched so fast and thoroughly.

As I opened my eyes with a violent start and resounding snort, I heard Jeff exclaim between peals of his and Ed's laughter, "What's the matter, Elyit, have a bad dream?"

Dreaming that wonderful bear chase, evidently I had been muttering in my sleep and Jeff and Ed, who were already up, had jerked the covers off and dashed a pail of ice cold water in my face. As I crawled out of the wet bed, mad enough to fight, Shep quit barking at our pack burro picketed down by the creek, and came to greet me with a tail wagging good morning. So the most exciting bear hunt I was ever on was ended by having cold water dashed on it just as it was about to come to a successful conclusion.

If the truth were known, we boys from the east side of the mountain had come to the Pecos high country to fish and not to hunt bear. The only suitable equipment we had for a bear hunt was Pa's .45-70, Model 1872, Winchester rifle. Jeff had a .32 rim fire rifle with which he shot a cock grouse for camp meat.

Jeff and Ed laughed so much all through breakfast at how surprised and ridiculous I had looked coming out of that bed, dripping wet, that I had to think up something to divert their attention. So I suggested we stage a fishing contest. We all three thought we were pretty darned good trout fishermen, each claiming to be able to beat the others. Jeff was a year older than I, while Ed and I were the same age, but Ed was handicapped because one leg was three or four inches shorter than the other. Just the same he got around mighty well with his hippity-hop gait when he was in a hurry.

"That's just fine," agreed Ed. "I'll beat you both in spite of my old leg."

"Fair enough. That's the only way to get it settled," said Jeff. Then as an afterthought, "but not today, let's wait 'till the day before we go home so we can take the fish home and not waste them."

"That's right, Mother would tan my hide, big as I am, if we let a lot of fish spoil," I said.

A fishing contest such as we had in mind, namely, to see how many fish we could catch in a given length of time, couldn't legally be put on today. There are bag limits, you know, but then there were none, or, if there were, we mountain boys had never heard of it.

When the eventful day arrived, we agreed to fish six hours, from eight o'clock in the morning until two in the afternoon. We would use artificial flies and no bait, and would keep no trout under six inches in length. The rivers were literally full of trout but rarely did we catch one over twelve inches. We would draw straws to see who fished where for the first hour or so. The short straw was for the Valdez Creek, the next for the Mora, and the long one for the river below the junction of the two streams. That was so we wouldn't get in each other's way at the start. After the first hour, we were all free to fish wherever we pleased.

It seems funny now, but in those days if there was another fisherman within a half-mile we thought the stream was overcrowded. We were to be back in the vicinity of camp by two o'clock, when Jeff, the timekeeper, since he was the only one who had a watch, would give the signal by yelling that it was time to quit. I don't now recall who drew which place to start fishing, but at eight o'clock sharp we were off with our two steel rods and a cheap bamboo. We each had an improvised burlap bag for a creel and when it got heavy with fish we transferred them to a willow stringer and cached them in some little pool at the edge of the stream to keep them fresh, where they would be picked up later.

The beautiful, gamey, red-bellied trout were striking anything we offered them. It's a good thing they did, too, for our assortment of flies then consisted, usually, of three or four kinds at most. A gray hackle with peacock body was always good, while the coachman ran it a close second. A brown hackle often got good results, and the royal coachman needed no apologies either. The cow dung and black gnat were others that we might occasionally get, but they weren't our regular offering.

If boys ever fished hard, we three rivals did it that day. If conditions for such a contest were ever better, I have never seen them. The sky was entirely clear until about eleven o'clock, then some thunder heads began showing up. By noon, it looked as if it would surely rain and spoil the rest of the day, but it only sprinkled a little and the clouds passed on. After that the trout struck with renewed enthusiasm as if they, too, were putting on a contest to see which could strike the fastest and hardest. Shades of Izaak Walton, what a day it was!

As two o'clock approached, we were all back near camp with our burlap creels bulging and willow stringers filled with trout but each still casting vigorously with aching arms lest the others would get ahead. The two o'clock yell was welcomed, for never had we fished so steadily or so earnestly, nor with the number of fish rather than sport as our objective.

We had taken no lunch and were right hungry but just had to count our trout to see who was the winner, before we cooked dinner. We all three counted each of the three batches of fish and you can bet we saw to it no mistakes were made. The results: Ed, 137; Elyit, as they called me, 148; and Jeff, 153. Game hogs, you say? Certainly, by today's standards, but forty-nine years ago there was not one fisherman in New Mexico where there are a hundred today, and, conversely, there were lots more fish then than now. Fisheries biologists would call a stream over-populated if they should be fortunate enough to find one that heavily stocked today.

After a very hearty dinner, mostly of yesterday's trout, had been cooked and eaten, we suddenly woke up to the fact that there were 438 trout to be cleaned and cared for. We wondered then if the contest had really been necessary after all, but having been brought up to waste no food, we set to work to do the long, tedious job.

Once the fish were cleaned and washed thoroughly, we dried them off inside and out with a dish towel which frequently had to be wrung out and dried by the campfire. The trout then were laid across some clean, dry aspen logs that we brought down from the hillside for the purpose. Laying out on these logs overnight the trout dried out thoroughly. In this high elevation, 9,500 feet, even in summertime the nights are chilly. By morning the fish were dry, cold, and crisp. Right after daylight, we placed them in the pack boxes between layers of green grass, and broke camp as early as we could. We arrived home by mid-afternoon with the fish still cool and crisp. There was feasting that night.

We mountain-raised boys of poor families were deprived of many of the pleasures and advantages which the city youngsters in better financial condition could enjoy and profit by. All that, I believe, was more than compensated for by the great privilege of making such incomparable trips as these into the wilderness. It is my fervent prayer that the Pecos Wilderness area may be perpetuated in its inspiring, pristine state so that our grandchildren and their children, down through the ages, may ha.ve the opportunity to enjoy and commune with nature there as has been my good fortune.

6

snowbound in the pecos high country

Don Juan Climaco Maestas, in 1872, when he was twenty-two years old, settled west of Rociada in a canyon which now bears his name. As a boy and young man I knew him well, for his place was only a few miles from our home on Sapello Creek. He had a little farm and some cattle, which, along with those of his neighbors, grazed in summer in the Pecos high country. Their particular range was in the Hamilton Mesa and Mora Flats area. On the mesa and in the mountain parks the full drooping heads of the mountain bunch grass were stirrup high, and the meadows were lush with tender, succulent forage and spangled with wild flowers.

Don Juan Climaco was quite a man. His neighbors, in their native tongue, referred to him as being *"muy hombrote."* He was tall, rawboned, and stout with keen, piercing black eyes. Besides being an unusually vigorous person and a good cowboy and woodsman, he always seemed just a little different from the other Spanish-speaking natives. Perhaps that was due to the fact that the Maestas family was not descended from any of the old original settlers but had come to New Mexico in about 1728 from Zacatecas, Mexico, and settled in the Santa Cruz Valley, near Española. A member of this original family, Phil Maestas, was a state senator from Rio Arriba County from 1949 to 1953.

Since Juan Climaco loved the Pecos high country, his neighbors usually arranged for him to look after their cattle and horses along with his own on the summer range, which lay across the high, rugged main range of the Sangre de Cristos from their ranches. So it was that he kept a summer camp at the Mora Flats or on the Rio Valdez across the ridge from Beatty's Cabin.

Juan Climaco rode with unusually long stirrups, even for a tall man, and his saddle was of the old-time rolled cantle and big flat horn type. It was an extraordinarily good saddle, for he bought it when he was twenty-one years old and used it all his life. The last horseback ride he took, not too long before he died, in 1929, was in this same old saddle. Of course, he had new stirrups and stirrup leathers, latigos, and lining every twenty or thirty years but, basically, it was the same old reliable saddle.

Once, when some folks I knew were camped in the Mora Flats on a fishing trip, they ran onto Juan Climaco up on top of Hamilton Mesa riding a snorty half-broke bronco. As is customary in breaking horses on the range, he was using a hacka-more instead of a bridle. Somehow, the throatlatch had come loose, which ordinarily would have made no difference at all but this time it was soon to get the rider into a serious predicament. The bronc was nervous and skittish as the group rode up. While they talked to Juan Climaco, someone's horse crowded up a little too close and a boot toe (I wouldn't want to admit it could have been mine) carelessly poked the bronc in the flank, and the merry-go-round started. That big roan bronc dropped his head and bucked and pitched and bawled like the very devil was in him. Juan Climaco's big black hat flew off the very first jump but he sat tight-legged in the long-stirruped saddle, one hand gripping the hackamore reins and the other arm swinging in rhythm with the bucking bronc's gyrations, like a hot jazz band leader's baton. That devilish bronco alternately pawed at the moon and rooted in the dirt, but Juan Climaco seemed to anticipate every twist and turn, utterly unperturbed at the hurricane which had so suddenly struck.

Long stirrups normally cause a rider to take much more punishment than shorter ones, but the way he sat the saddle, foretelling every move the horse made, was proof of his master horsemanship. Then the bronc came down out of the sky stiff-legged and hard, head between his knees and, since the throat-latch was loose, the hackamore was jarred off over his ears. Not only was Juan Climaco left on his perilous perch without any means of control, but the threshing about of the hackamore headstall beneath the horse's breast seemed to scare him more at every jump. The headstall got tangled in the bronc's feet and the reins were jerked out of the buckaroo's hands. Then he was on his own for sure.

Now that the big roan was entirely loose, it is the greatest wonder in the world that he didn't run away and drag the rider off in the nearby spruce forest. Fortunately, he preferred to exert every effort to throw Juan right there. He bucked high and came down hard; he reared and plunged and bawled; he twisted and whirled in the air; he sunfished first one way and then the other, but all in vain, for Juan Climaco rode without reins as if he were glued to the saddle. It was the doggonedest Wild West show those mountains had ever witnessed.

It must have been like the description a cowboy once gave of a bad bronco he had ridden, when he said, "That son-of-a-jumpin' kangaroo got his tail between his teeth and took lockjaw. The harder he bit, the worse it hurt, and the worst it hurt, the madder he got, which, altogether, gave him the excuse to chin a cloud and come down stiff-legged, all four feet on a spot no bigger'n a Dutch oven. Then he would wipe out his tracks with first one of my stirrups and then the other. He shore jarred every bone in my body, which is what he set out to do in the first place, but, durn his snakey hide, I rid him."

Now about the hardest and most exhausting work a horse can do is to get down and do a right good job of bucking, and the hardest work a man can do is to ride a hard-bucking horse. The show couldn't last long; something had to give, but it wasn't the rider this time. Gradually, the wild-eyed horse began to tire, his tempo slowed down and his vigor was gone, the jumps were not so high nor so crooked. His head gradually came up and he goat-jumped around for a brief moment. Then, eyes blazing with anger and fright, sides heaving, and nostrils flaring, he came to a trembling stop. He had had enough. Juan Climaco was a bit pale and very much out of wind, too, but he had made the bronc say, "Uncle."

"*Que chivato!*" he exclaimed. Then slowly he unbuckled the rope strap on the side of the saddle, took lariat in hand, opened a small noose and, with great care, slowly eased it over the bronc's head, patted him soothingly on the neck, and got off. The bronc snorted and backed away but stopped when the rope around his neck tightened. Hat and hackamore were gathered up and brought to the victorious rider, who was still breathing hard but was as calm as if nothing had happened. Keeping the rope tight, he slowly walked up to the bronc, who eyed him half defiantly, half respectfully, and patted him on nose and neck. *"Por Dios, que tienes? Ya sabes que no puedes tumbarme."* "By God, what's the matter with you? You know you can't throw me." Then he gently put the hackamore back on, tied the throatlatch securely, replaced his lariat, and remounted the trembling, sweat-lathered bronco as unconcernedly as I would get on the gentlest saddle horse. The roan was no longer just half-broke.

In the Pecos high country, cattle and horses are rounded up in October, at the latest, and driven out of the mountains to the home ranches, where they spend the winter or are marketed. To linger later is to risk getting snowed in. When snow comes in the high country, cattle will naturally drift down into lower ranges to get out of it. Not so with horses; instead, they will often go on even higher and injudiciously try to winter there. That trait often gets them into serious trouble, as their gruesome carcasses sometimes bear witness after snows have melted and the yards where they starved to death are found.

In the fall of 1907, a dozen or so horses belonging to Juan Climaco Maestas and his neighbors were not to be found when the other stock was rounded up and driven in. Since there were a couple of old gentle work mares in the bunch, it was thought they would lead the others over the range to the ranch in due time. The snows came early but no horses showed up. November came, bringing more heavy snows and driving winds, but still no horses and the owners began to worry about their safety.

December came, with more snow and drifts piled high, but no horses. By the middle of the month, Juan Climaco decided it was high time to do something about the situation, despite the frowning 11,500-foot, snow-packed range that he would have to cross. He well knew what he was going up against, for, even as late as June; he often had to maneuver his cattle around the deep drifts near the summit to get across to the summer range. His family and neighbors tried to discourage him. The horses probably had found a place to winter, they argued. But, even if they hadn't, what of it, what were a few head of horses compared to risking one's life in the unfriendly snowdrifts?

"Dejalos alii, si los hallamos en la primavera estd bien, y si no los hallamos poco se pierde," "Leave them there, if we find them in the spring, fine; if not what's the difference," they said. But Juan Climaco would have none of it, and it is certain that his decision to try to rescue those horses was not based on mercenary consideration. His love of horses and the thought of them yarding up in the deep snow and starving to death impelled him to make the desperate effort, against great odds, to find them and bring them out.

It would be almost foolhardy to go alone, but who would go with him? Then, inspired by his determination, two neighbors, Pablo Herrera and Cornelio Trujillo, who owned some of the missing horses, reluctantly agreed to go. So it was that, about December 18, the three set out on their stoutest saddle horses leading two pack animals, one loaded with grain for their mounts and the other with light camp equipment and provisions for a week for themselves.

The long 4,000-foot climb to the top of the range was a grueling test of horseflesh. The snow was a foot deep at the ranch and grew steadily deeper as they approached the crest, until it was breast deep to the horses, who could hardly plow through it even a few yards at a time. Near the crest, where the strong winter blasts swept the snow off the open top of the Primer Bordo, they hit drifts piled ten to fifteen feet deep, and had to work their way around them and up through wind-swept alleys between the huge snow piles. Often the crusted drifts were too tough for the horses to plunge through at all, and the three men took turns tramping out a path for them.

It had taken them almost all day to come the five miles, but when someone suggested that it might be well to turn back Juan Climaco chose not to hear; instead, he redoubled his efforts to break through the last snow barrier. The others followed. At long last, just before sundown, they got through to the top, and, in the face of a sharp freezing winter wind, looked across the vast expanse of snow-blanketed ridges and canyons, somewhere among which they hoped to find their lost horses.

On top, except for the bitter cold wind, the going was good, for the persistent winds had swept the snow off to pile up the formidable drifts through which they had so laboriously fought their way. They made fair time, and, by dark, had gotten well down into the Rito Del Oso. Here, near where Professor Dyche had made his camp while hunting grizzly bear twenty-five years before, they made a snowy camp in a sheltered spot under a clump of spruce trees.

Next morning they set out again and slowly plowed through the deep, soft snow in the timbered canyons to the Mora Flats, at the junction of Rio Mora and Rio Valdez. They had hoped to find some sign of the horses here but were doomed to disappointment. Hamilton Mesa was the next objective, for there is where the horses ranged in summer and it seemed likely they might be there, living on one of the wind-swept areas where some grass would be exposed for food. After a tough climb through the two- to three-foot deep snow, with a hard crust here on the more open south exposures, they reached the top of the mesa and again were sorely disappointed at not finding any sign at all. The mesa is a big area and they determined to cover it all and find the horses if they were there. After riding a mile or so, toward the south end of the Mesa, they stopped to discuss again plans for the hunt. Here they were in an excellent position to look across the main Pecos Canyon and see the slopes of Round Mountain and the many parks all the way around to Beatty's Cabin.

Suddenly Juan Climaco exclaimed, *"A Hi estdn, alii estdn los caballos!"* and sure enough, there they were yarded up at the edge of the big Beatty Park two miles, as the crow flies, across the deep canyon. Most fortunately, the horses had yarded in a spot where they could be seen, for there are hundreds of places where they might have been caught entirely out of sight. Now that the horses had been located, the next question was how to get to them and get them out.

Juan Climaco led the way through the timber down an old trail, which hits the canyon a half-mile below Beatty's Cabin. It was just about dark and there was no chance of getting to the horses that night, so they sought out a place to spend another cold night. They picked a spot under a ledge of rock, about two hundred yards from where the new Beatty's Cabin is now situated. In this protected nook, with a big campfire, they were able to make themselves fairly comfortable. Even the tired horses were able to paw down through the snow on the steep, grassy hillside and get a little grass to supplement the grain ration.

At the crack of dawn the three woodsmen set out on their stoutest horses to make the rescue. It is a curious fact that horses will yard up and stay in a small, tramped-down area and starve to death when, if they would, they could break through the breast-high snow and get out. Once a track is broken, they will follow it to safety. In this instance, when the first big snows came, they probably had continued to graze in the big park, on the steep hillside, where the snow would not lay as deep as in the timber, even though they had to paw down to the grass. Then when another big storm came and they tried to leave, they hit the very deep snow in the timber at the edge of the park, started milling around, and, before they knew it, had made a small yard and refused to break out of it.

These Beatty's Park slopes are snowy and the men found the going tough from the very start. There was no cut-out trail, and in the timbered part of the slope the rescuers not only had the deep snow to contend with but many log barriers as well. Perhaps, in their anxiety, they crowded their mounts too hard for, when within a couple of hundred yards of their destination, the horses refused to budge further up the steep hill, where they had to lunge their way through if they made any headway at all. So the horses were left and the three men took turns breaking trail literally a foot at a time. After a while, they came in sight of their quarry amazingly gaunt and emaciated. As they approached the rim of the tramped-out yard, the starving animals whinnied repeatedly to their rescuers. Then Juan Climaco exclaimed, *"Mira los pobrecitos!"* "See the poor things!" as he noticed that they had eaten off all the hair from each other's manes and tails. Not only that, but the few spruce and aspen trees in reach had the bark of trunk and limbs eaten off as if a giant porcupine had been at work. Only two months before they had all been fat as butter and sleek as seals.

When the trail was opened into the snow-walled corral, it was to be expected that the old, gentle horses would crowd and nuzzle their rescuers; but these experienced horsemen were astounded to find the unbroken young horses just as gentle and entirely without fear. The problem now was to keep from being trampled to death in the snow by the anxiously crowding animals. At first they had to fight them off with clubs but, finally, they got one of the old mares started down the trail which they had so tediously broken coming up, and the others followed, hungrily biting off and eating the ends of green spruce boughs as they went.

At camp, the remainder of the oats was divided between the starving horses and their own mounts and the long trek back to the ranch was begun. Following the path they had broken, the going was nothing like as tedious as it had been coming over. Juan Climaco led the way and the others followed to drive the loose horses, but there was no need of that for they followed like dogs all the way. They planned to camp on the Rito Del Oso, but when they got there, at dusk, the clouds had banked in and another snowstorm seemed imminent. Juan Climaco knew that the Pecos high country was no place to be caught in a snowstorm in December, so, despite the fact that the three men, as well as their mounts and the emaciated remuda, were about all in, they pushed slowly on, reaching the ranch well after midnight.

In telling me about this trip, some years later, Don Juan Climaco, wonderful mountaineer, cowboy, and rancher that he was, said it was the toughest job, with the most gratifying outcome, of anything he had ever undertaken.

If it seems a bit silly for range horses to get caught by Old Man Winter and lose, or come near losing, their lives by failing to come out in time, let us remember that there are many cases on record where men have been caught in like manner, sometimes perishing, and at other times coming perilously near it. More than one near tragedy has occurred right there in the beautiful, but treacherous, Pecos high country. Mrs. Fred Robinson recently told me of one instance, which occurred in 1896, when she was a small girl living with her mother and stepfather at a place just above Cowles, which later became known as the old Club House, a dozen miles downstream from Beatty's Cabin.

It seems two old prospectors, Sullivan and Williams, with packs on their backs, went into the Beatty's Cabin area in the fall to search for gold. They had no tent and only a couple of blankets each for bedding, and, naturally, their food supply of sow belly, flour, beans, sugar, salt, and coffee was quite limited. With fishhooks and a rifle, they were able for a time to supplement their meager larder. The snows came early, one after another, but, with the gold fever in their veins, they lingered on, hoping the weather would clear and they would strike it rich before winter set in, in earnest. Their food supply was running out and their camp was wholly inadequate, but, worst of all, they little realized how quickly the Pecos high country can be transformed from pleasant fall to arctic winter and become a perilous place.

After two weeks of wintry weather, they went out in search of game for food, plodding through the snow, which was already knee deep, but not a track could they find. Game had been smarter than they. Bear had hibernated, grouse had taken to the dense spruce trees, where they could not be found, and deer had drifted down into the lower country to spend the winter. Thus, all possibility of replenishing their larder was eliminated. Returning, after two days of hard hunting, empty-handed and, incidentally, with equally empty bellies, they suddenly realized that there was only flour enough left for a couple of tortillas. They determined to head for the ranch next morning.

They were a day too late. That night the storm broke again, raging in over the towering Truchas Peaks upon them. For two days and nights the snow fell, piling two feet more on top of what they already had, and the wind whipped up huge drifts here and there throughout the area. It would have been suicide to start out in the storm, so they waited, with hunger gnawing ever harder at their bellies, in their snowy camp protected from the wintry blasts only by a crudely built brush wall under a clump of spruce trees. Weakened by cold and hunger, the task of getting wood enough to keep the all-important campfire going became a desperately real problem.

Down at the ranch, a dozen miles below, Mrs. Robinson's mother, Mrs. Hume, a very thoughtful lady who was always most solicitous for the welfare of others, and one who knew the Pecos high country as few other women have known it, became increasingly worried for the safety of the two old prospectors. When they didn't show up by evening of the day after the terrific storm broke, she insisted that her son, Alfred Viles (later widely known as Skipper Viles), and Tom Stewart go in search of the prospectors. She knew there was something wrong and that they needed help. The young men were about nineteen and twenty-one years old, strong and mountain raised. So they set out at break of day, afoot, with very light packs on their backs, to plod their way through the deep snow to look for the lost prospectors. They couldn't make it up over Round Mountain but worked their tedious way up the river for a couple of miles, then climbed part way out of the canyon and followed a route around the hillside through the timber toward Beatty's Cabin. Some of the drifts were so deep they could not plow through them, but, fortunately, the crust was hard enough to hold them up when they lay flat on their bellies. Thus, they literally wormed their way over several of these snow-packed barriers.

When they were within three miles of Beatty's, they began yelling loudly every little while trying to locate the prospectors' camp. Soon they got an answer, and, before long, made contact with Williams, who was trying to come out. He told them his partner was too weak to try it and had stayed in camp hoping that help could be sent in for him. The young men gave the famished Williams something to eat and a nip from the bottle they had brought along, and sent him on to the ranch in the path they had broken through the snow, while they plowed on to the sorry winter camp where Sullivan was holed up. Arriving just before dark, they found the old prospector chewing on an empty sugar sack trying to get a little nourishment out of it. He was indeed in a bad way, cold, hungry, and dirty. He gradually gained some strength as they gave him just a little food at a time throughout the long, cold night.

As soon as it was light enough to travel, they started back. The old fellow was still mighty weak and had to be helped and urged on continually. There was a little whiskey left in the bottle and Sullivan begged them for a big drink of it but they would not give it to him. "The only way we could get him to travel at all was by promising him a little nip every half mile," Alfred said, in telling about it. "Never did anyone work so hard for so little."

They were on the last leg of the journey when the whiskey played out, but, at last, they reached the ranch to find plenty of food and warm beds. A tragedy had been avoided by the thoughtfulness of a good woman and the good sense and stout sinews of two young mountain men.

7

lion hunting on the pecos

One clear, crisp morning in October, 1911, I left the Panchuela Ranger Station on Nig, an obstreperous but sturdy saddle horse, and, leading Buck, packed with my camp outfit, headed for the Pecos high country. From camp at Beatty's Cabin, I expected to spend a week riding the surrounding area to oversee the rounding up and removal of livestock from the high summer grazing ranges to farms and ranches on the east side of the mountain. Stock was grazed there in the lush parks and meadows of the Pecos high country under Forest Service permit for a specific period in summer, and it was one of my duties as district ranger to see that the permittees removed their stock on schedule.

As we topped out at the big blow-out below the corral on Round Mountain, I noticed a mountain lion scrape beside the trail. A little further on was another scrape, indicating the lion was traveling in the same general direction that I was. Lion scrapes are made by short, heavy, alternating, backward strokes of* the lion's hind feet, leaving a short dual dig, with debris and dirt pushed up from three to six inches high behind it, and indicates definitely which way the lion is traveling. The scrapes are the male lion's scent station or marker, but seldom, if ever, are they made by the female. While these scrapes were, perhaps, two days old, I wished for a good pack of hounds to put on the trail. I had no dogs of my own at that time, although I had been raised hunting mountain lions and bobcats with dogs, which is one of the finest and most thrilling of sports.

Five miles farther on, where the trail passes the top of the high cliffs which form a box canyon a mile below Beatty's Cabin, there was a very fresh lion scrape beside an old rotten log. Half buried by the little, scraped-up heap of tree needles and rotted wood was a pile of fresh dung, black as tar, a sure sign the lion had been gorging himself on fresh meat. Closer inspection of the scat proved that the meat had been that of a deer, for there was plenty of deer hair mixed in. Now, for sure, I longed for hounds, or any good trail dog, for it was almost certain the lion was close by.

Just before I got to the forks of the river at Beatty's Cabin a pair of ravens flew up from a willow patch near the stream. At once, I suspected they had located the lion's deer kill, which, upon riding down to the spot, proved to be right. There in the willows was the fresh carcass of a big doe pretty well covered over with grass and sticks that the lion had scraped up from all sides. The mountain lion covers his kill when he leaves it, to keep it fresh and protect it from birds and animals. He also rips open the belly and removes the stomach and intestines, which he rarely ever eats; but he does' nearly always eat the liver, heart, and kidneys. This one had done just that and had also eaten a big chunk of meat out of the brisket area, which is also standard practice. The teats and udder showed the doe had been suckling a fawn which, being left alone, would almost certainly fall prey to some predator.

Camp was made beside a big, seven-foot-high, square-topped boulder in the middle of the park above the old Beatty Cabin site. I chose this location so that I could put my camp outfit on top of the rock while I was away, to keep cattle from messing it up, as they might do in search of salt. My horses were picketed nearby, for lions are particularly fond of horse flesh. The lion returned to his kill the first night and made another big meal off of it, covered it over and then abandoned it entirely. Later that fall, H. S. Arnold, my father-in-law and owner of the Bar N Cattle and Horse Ranch, on Chaparrito and Cow creeks, at the southeast edge of the Pecos high country, had some colts killed by lions and asked Supervisor Tom Stewart to send me over to try to kill the marauding lions. Neither Stewart nor I had any hunting dogs, but we promised to try to locate a pack and help him out. It was not until about the first of February that we got around to it and, meanwhile, several more of his colts had been killed. Lewellen Loyd, a Scotchman who winter-grazed some cattle and a few horses in Holy Ghost Canyon, also reported a brood mare and colt killed by a lion. I wondered if my big Beatty's Cabin lion had tired of venison and turned horse killer.

S. L. Fisher, an old friend of mine who lived on the east side of the range between Tecolote and Gallinas creeks, had a very fine pack of hounds and was a mighty good lion hunter. Mrs. Fisher, who handled all of his correspondence for him, wrote, in response to my inquiry, that Mr. Fisher would be very glad to go with me for ten days or two weeks, but that I would have to come over to "work out some details." We had moved from Panchuela Ranger Station to Santa Fe for the winter, so I left my pretty young wife there and made the two-day horseback ride to Fisher's Ranch via Pecos and the Big Cross Trail. Fisher, who loved lion hunting as well as I did, was rarin' to go, but Mrs. Fisher wouldn't let him until I promised her that I would keep him out in the country the whole time, away from any town or village. Understanding her reasons, I promised.

Next morning Fisher and I left at crack of dawn, despite near zero weather, rode to Gallinas Creek and up it, heading for the Bar N Ranch via the Elk Mountain Trail. The three long-eared hounds which we brought along ranged in front of us, while we led a pack horse loaded with some grain for the horses, dog food, a little emergency grub, and a light bedroll, just in case we should have to lay out overnight. Ordinarily, it would be impossible to cross the Elk Mountain Trail in February, but the snowfall had been exceptionally light and we thought we could make it. We were sadly mistaken. The drifts in the old burn on the east crest of the range were ten feet deep and we could find no way to get through them. We turned back down the Burro Basin for a little way, then, our horses, floundering through the deep-crusted snow, cut across to the dense forest on the south side of it. There the snow was still deep but soft and not drifted at all and we finally worked—and I mean worked—our way to the top of the range, a mile or more south of Elk Mountain. It was well along in the afternoon by then and the ten-mile route to the Arnold Ranch didn't look good at all, so we decided to try to go south, down the high divide to the Tracy Ranch, on the head of Bull Creek.

What a trip it was I Soft, deep snow in the heavy timber to wallow through, crusted drifts to dodge at the edges of the parks and old burns, and a little open ground on the barren, windswept ridges, where the frozen ground was slick as glass. The poor hounds often could hardly make it even in the path opened by our horses, but they fared better at the drifts because they could walk on top of the crust. No lion sign at all was seen.

It was getting dark when we got to the Tracy Ranch, where we were received with typical Western hospitality, and our horses and dogs, as well as ourselves, were mighty well taken care of for the night. We were told some lion signs had been seen in the vicinity earlier in the winter but none for some time past. Our hopes of picking up a good trail and catching a lion enroute to the Arnold Ranch were not very bright.

At sunrise next morning we set out over a trail toward the Frank Emerson Ranch, on Manzanares Creek. No sooner had we crossed the ridge and started down a side canyon a mile from the house than business began to pick up. Fannie, the fine little Redbone, black and tan strike dog, who was ranging off to our right, suddenly opened with a long-drawn-out, high-pitched bellow that made the woods ring. Fisher said, "She's hit a hot one, let's go!" Ed, a big, stout, red hound, dashed across the trail ahead of us with Drum, an equally big, black-and-tan hound, close on his heels, to join their little dependable partner. They knew that when Fannie spoke in that tone of voice it meant urgent business. Fannie repeated her first signal, then set out on the trail and, as Ed and Drum joined her, the woods reverberated with the sweetest music that can come to a lion hunter's ears.

Fisher, mounted on Old Turk, a great mountain horse, was instantly off after the pack in a high lope through the brush and timber down the trailless canyon. In those good old days, I had the reputation of being able to ride with the toughest and most reckless brush riders. But this time, damn it, I was leading the pack horse and Fisher rode right off and left me. For a little while he was able to keep in sight of the baying hounds and enjoy watching them unravel that lion trail in high gear, but, before long, they jumped their quarry and left him behind, too. It was all I could do to keep in hearing of the pack as it gave tongue freely and excitedly on the hot trail.

Once I stopped to listen for a few seconds, and, in that instant, caught the change that had taken place. The baying was sharper, with shorter choppy notes and even higher pitched. I knew the pack was barking "treed." As I hurried on, dragging the pack horse after me, a shot rang out and, since Fisher was an excellent shot, I knew we -had a lion. I hurried on as fast as I could, although there was no need of hurrying now. Then I became puzzled, for the hounds were still barking "treed" even more vigorously than before, when they should be silently wooling the dead lion down the hillside.

When I rode up, the puzzling situation was revealed. There was the lion, a fair-sized male, hanging by a hind leg from a limb high in the yellow pine tree. Fisher had shot him through the heart and, as the lion fell off the big limb backwards, a hind leg had caught under one limb and over another. There he hung, the leverage against the joint and the leg straight and stiff.

"Can you shin up that tree?" Fisher asked.

"I doubt it," I replied, "It is too far to the first limb."

"Well, I sure can't on account of this old leg of mine."

Fisher had sustained a badly broken leg in a fall with a horse, and it was crooked and he limped when he walked; besides, he was past fifty years old.

"How we goin' to get him down?" Fisher asked.

"Shoot him down," I said.

"Like hell you will, them limbs is three inches thick."

"Want to bet?"

Without waiting for his answer, I pulled my .32 Winchester Special rifle from the saddle scabbard, took careful aim, squeezed off the trigger, and down came the big, long-tailed cat.

"I'll be damned," exclaimed Fisher, "I would have bet you Old Turk against that stove-up nag of yours, you couldn't do it."

I had seen that if the lion's leg could be broken between the two limbs that were holding it, it would release the leverage and come loose and with a lucky shot, that is what it did. We threw the lion on top of the pack, rode to the Emerson Ranch, where we stopped for coffee and a brief visit, and then on to the Arnold Bar N Ranch by way of Valle del Osha and Cow Creek, in time for a late dinner. The Arnolds were even more pleased than we that one colt-killer had been taken so quickly.

During the several days that we spent at the Arnold Ranch, we were taken care of royally. The dogs had a good place to sleep, the horses were stabled and well fed, and we were given fresh horses to ride whenever we wanted them. Never were two hunters pampered so much and, as it turned out, we accomplished very little, at the time, to compensate for it.

With high hopes, we set out the first morning, going up around Pannel Creek and the rough country at the lower end of Soldier Creek. The south slopes were mostly barren of snow and terribly slick, making it almost impossible for the horses, even though sharp shod, to keep their footing on the steep grassy hillsides. The north exposures had some snow, which, of course, became deeper as we got into higher country. It seems to me both Emery and Charles Arnold went with us and we rode hard all day. We went up to the head of Soldier Creek, then across to the mouth of Elk Creek, and down Cow Creek, then up through the Rincon and back to Cow Creek again, arriving back at the ranch house at dusk. In all the distance we never picked up any fresh lion sign at all. We did see a few very old scrapes in the general area where some colts had been killed earlier in the season, but nothing that Fannie thought worthwhile.

For four days, we rode out the whole area in every direction, with exactly no results whatever. Could it be there had been only one lion in the country, doing all that damage? Surely, there was a female somewhere there, as well as more males, but we couldn't find track nor scrape.

Wounded Lion Jumps Out

On the evening of the fourth day, Fisher decided he had to go home for a day or two, so on the fifth morning we set out early, planning to go back by way of Emerson's and Tracy's ranches, as we had come over, but, from Tracy's, we would take the trail over the divide and down the Tecolote Creek. By noon we were at Tracy's, and, early in the afternoon, as we approached the top of the range, Fannie gave tongue a time or two as she sniffed the crusted snow on which she was walking. Evidently, the scent was faint and we suspected it was a bobcat track, but we couldn't see a print of any kind.

Pretty soon we passed out of the open country into the heavy spruce timber, where the snow was soft. We got a glimpse of a big trail, where something had broken through after leaving the crusted snow, and knew at once it was no bobcat. As soon as the dogs reached the spot, they instantly came alive and set off in full cry, as fast as they could encumbered by the two-foot snow.

"It's a lion!" exclaimed Fisher, and the hounds confirmed it over and over again, emphatically, positively.

The mysteries of trail scent are many. Often the ability of a good, cold-nosed dog to work an old, difficult trail is miraculous. Fannie had been known to give tongue freely on a two-weeks-old lion track frozen in the snow. Yet here she had barely been able to pick up the faintest kind of scent, from the moist surface of the crusted snow, of a track which proved to be only two or three hours old at most. Ed and Drum never indicated that they had the slightest suspicion that a lion had gone that way, but at the spot where the lion had left the hard surface and bogged down in the soft snow, the scent was pungent and inspiring.

This time we both were able to keep up with the hounds, for we had no pack horse. Besides, the hounds could not make much time because of the deep snow. This time big Ed took the lead, with Drum right on his heels. Fannie's feelings were hurt because, on account of her short legs and slight frame, she was unable to keep up. Her usual melodious baying on a trail was now more of a whimper and complaining barking, but Ed and Drum made up for it. Their voices were musical, full of intense excitement and anticipation.

The lion track bore to the northeast, angling away from the Tecolote Trail, but we cared not at all, for it was a wonderful chase. We gradually fell behind the lead dogs and they got a quarter of a mile or more ahead of us, not because our horses were unable to keep up but because Fannie couldn't and we refused to humiliate her further by getting ahead of her. After a couple of miles, we thrilled as one always does when the dogs bark "treed." Fannie recognized the change of tone and staccato barking, too, and put forth every possible effort to get to the tree in a hurry.

The spruce timber was dense and we were right close before we could see Mr. Long Tail, but there he was, not fifteen feet off the ground, panting hard from his run through the snow. A beautiful specimen he was, too, reddish-yellow sides, slightly darker back, snow-white belly, and a big, round head with gray markings. I got off to shoot him and he was close enough so I should have been able to shoot an eye out.

"Shoot him through the heart so as not to spoil the skull," Fisher cautioned me.

"O. K., that will be easy."

We both knew that a wounded lion let down among the pack can do irreparable damage. Why I did it, I don't know, but I had kept the end of the bridle reins in my right hand, with which I held the forearm of the rifle, as I shoot left-handed. At the instant I pulled the trigger, Nig threw his head up and jerked the rifle off line, and the lion came out of the tree with only a front leg broken, up near his body.

Fisher didn't say a word, but I would ten times rather he had cursed me out and knocked me down, which I deserved, than to have had to take the contemptuous look he gave me. Fortunately, the lion took a few long, fast leaps, despite his broken leg, and the dogs didn't catch him on the ground. He treed again within a hundred yards. I asked Fisher if he wanted to do the shooting this time and he said, "No! But by God, I'll hold your damn horse."

We carried the lion, which was a normal-sized mature male, back of Fisher's saddle to the trail, gutted him there, and hung him up to be picked up on our trip back to the Arnold Ranch. It was late when we got to the Fisher Ranch, but, as if by mental telepathy, Mrs. Fisher said she was expecting us, and soon had a very fine beefsteak supper ready. After a day's rest, we went back to the Arnold Bar N Ranch, taking our lion with us to prove we were paying for our keep.

A Quickie At Loyd's Ranch

We spent one day there hunting but, as before, could turn up nothing at all. During the day, Lewellen Loyd had phoned that his *vaquero* had just seen some old lion sign up the Holy Ghost Canyon. That was enough; we phoned back that we would be there by sunrise next morning. So the three of us, Fisher, Emery Arnold, and I, ate breakfast by lamplight and were in the saddles before daylight. The five-mile trip, by mountainous trail, to the Loyd Ranch at the mouth of the Holy Ghost Canyon, was bitter cold, but we arrived even earlier than we had promised. Loyd hadn't had breakfast yet, and I wanted to hurry on because I knew if we lingered at all he would offer us a drink, and that Fisher couldn't refuse the first, much less the second, and the hunt would be spoiled.

So we agreed that we would go on to cut sign and that Loyd and his *vaquero* would follow and catch us in time to be in on the kill, if any. We hadn't gone a half-mile up the canyon when we saw a big streak of blood on the snow in the canyon bottom. At the same instant, the three hounds, who were ahead of us, scented something and took off across the canyon at top speed, heads up and bellowing like they were after the devil himself. Loping over to the blood stains, I saw it was where a lion had just dragged a deer, which he evidently had killed up on the barren south exposure, across the canyon to the snowy side in the brush.

By that time the hounds barked "treed" not over a hundred yards up the slope. Emery and I got off our horses and went afoot up that way and soon spied a big male lion thirty feet up a tall Douglas fir tree. He was clinging to the body of the tree, looking down at the baying hounds as if undecided whether to go on up to some comfortable limbs or to jump out and try to make his getaway. We didn't give him time to make up his mind. Emery took my .32 Winchester Special, which hangs over my desk as I write this, and put a bullet squarely through his shoulders. The dogs worried the carcass down to the canyon bottom and saved us the trouble of going up after it.

We put the lion across my saddle and tied it there, and I led my horse back to the house. Loyd was at breakfast and his cowboy was just saddling their horses. Never have I seen a man more surprised and pleased than the old Scotchman. In his rich Scotch brogue, he sputtered over his words worse than ever. We had to have coffee and rolls and then, despite the time of day, the Scotch and soda were brought out. I tried to stop it but couldn't and, although Emery and I didn't indulge at all, Fisher and Loyd soon were reminiscing intimately. It seems Loyd formerly had been foreman of the W. S. Ranch, near Cimarron, and they had a lot of mutual friends, including the Scotch.

We all rode out for just a little while that afternoon, not far, but we did see a nice bunch of wild turkeys, and a mule deer doe with a pair of yearlings. That night Loyd and Fisher really became bosom pals. Next morning, I was successful in getting Loyd to tell Fisher he was all out of liquor, hadn't a drop left in the house, a bloody shame you know. (He eased his conscience by not considering the basement a part of the house.) When that was settled, we rode two and a half miles down to Indian Creek, then up it and over the trail toward the head of El Macho Canyon. There we found plenty of lion sign and it looked as if we were in for some more good luck. We had taken three mature male lions with a minimum of effort. In each instance, the hot trail had been picked up at an unexpected moment and the chases were far shorter and easier than is usual. Would we have like experience here in the Indian Creek-Macho Canyon country?

The Old Long-Tailed Traveler

We worked up the ridge between Indian Creek and the east fork of Macho, where we found plenty of lion scrapes, some fresh enough for Fannie to talk to, but the trail was too old to be worked out. Finally, near some old prospect holes, we did strike a track that the dogs could handle, although slowly, as it was, perhaps, two days old. Wherever there was soft snow they did fine, but on the barren south exposures it was difficult and in places where the big cat had walked on the crusted snow they were stymied. The hounds worked beautifully in their diligent efforts to make headway. Ed and Drum put implicit trust in Fannie and never questioned her decisions. When little Fannie gave tongue, they knew she had the trail and, without going to her to verify it, they would range on ahead to try to pick up the scent farther on. Not so, Fannie. She did not reciprocate their confidence. Instead, when either Ed or Drum barked on the trail, although ever so confidently, Fannie would go to him, check the scent herself, and make sure to her own personal olfactory satisfaction that old long tail had gone that way, then proclaim it with a long drawn-out bawl before venturing on ahead.

We crossed the east fork of Macho Creek high up, and then the trail turned southward, paralleling it. For a while we made better time, as it was more shaded here, but we still were able to ride right behind the hounds and enjoy, to the fullest, the inspiring thrill of watching them work. Although the teamwork was a bit one-sided, it was marvelous to watch, nevertheless. When, at last, we crossed the south fork and headed on southward, the sun was low over the mountain to the west. The prospects were not good for catching up before dark. It was a long way back to Loyd's, and, despite the fact there was little snow for the time of year, the nights were mighty cold to lay out in, to get an early start on the trail, as both Fisher and I had done before and I have done since.

The trail led southward and then began circling a little to the east, through timbered mesa land. Just at sundown, we came to a fenced-in opening where there had been an oat field and a little potato patch, which we had not known were up there. A trail led away from it down a draw and we suspected there would be a prospector's cabin down there. Fisher blew his cow's-horn and called the dogs off, and, following the path, we soon came to a pretty good log cabin, but no one was home. Evidently the owner, who, we later learned, was an old Frenchman who had some mining claims nearby, had moved out for the winter. In a shed was stacked a ton or so of bundled oat hay—just what we needed for the horses. There was also a little half-dug-out potato cellar locked up tight; hence, we guessed there were potatoes in it.

The cabin was also locked with a heavy padlock, and the lone window had bars across it and was boarded up on the inside. Through a crack we could see there was a stove and some bedding and, possibly, some provisions inside. It is axiomatic among the good country people of the West that a traveler in need of shelter and food for the night is welcome whether or not anyone is home. It was nearly dark and getting colder by the minute, and we were tired and hungry and it was a long way back to Loyd's. Besides, if we were to catch that lion on the morrow, we had need to be right here at daybreak. So we decided to stay all night, even though the latchstring didn't hang on the outside.

I undertook to open the locked door, while Emery and Fisher unsaddled and fed the horses. They then pulled the hasp and opened the potato cellar and found an abundance of Irish potatoes. The lock on the door of the house was a big, old-style padlock, connecting the ends of a chain run through a hole in the heavy, homemade door, and around the door frame, locking it firmly. It was a difficult job for a novice in such matters but, at last, the lock sprung open undamaged. No, I will not tell you how it was done for some reader might be tempted to use the same method for a less worthy purpose.

But the door wouldn't open. It was securely barred on the inside. We searched diligently but could find no string or wire or latch on the outside anywhere to manipulate it. We had the alternative of spending the night huddled together in the little potato cellar or breaking the door down. We were debating which to do, when, to light a cigarette, Emery struck a match on the end of a log at the corner of the cabin and a piece of clay mortar as big as your hand fell to the ground. The end of a heavy flat iron bar, made from an old wagon tire, was thus inadvertently exposed. It had been pushed in through a slot in the log, chiseled out to fit, across the door and into a bracket on the other side, thus barring the door completely. We pulled the long bar out, opened the door, and went inside.

We soon had a roaring fire going in the iron cook stove, cleaned up the place a bit, and got supper. Supper, by the way, and breakfast, too, for that matter, consisted of French fried potatoes, boiled potatoes, baked potatoes and mashed potatoes, for the only grub we found was a can of bacon grease, some salt and a cellar full of potatoes. The hounds had the same fare we did. There were only a couple of old blankets and a homemade sugan and straw mattress so we didn't sleep much. We were warm and well fed, after a fashion, our horses and dogs pretty well cared for, and we were where we wanted to be at daylight, so we had no complaint. Next morning, we left as much or more stove wood and kindling as we found there, left a five dollar bill in a can, labeled "open," on the table, locked and barred the cabin and cellar just as we had found them, and left an unsigned note of thanks for the accommodations. We were ready to hit the lion trail again by sunrise.

Emery never was too enthusiastic about hunting of any kind, so he decided he had had enough and left us, to ride back to the Bar N Ranch. You couldn't have pried Fisher and me off that trail by any means; that chase had been started and, at all costs, must be finished. A fifteen-minute ride and we were back on the trail of old long tail, and the canyons were again reverberating with the melodious baying of the pack. The trail led into lower country, where there was little or no snow, but very slick hillsides. The big old lion was hunting and the trail meandered around the rough places, with no set course. For hours the hounds worked diligently but made slow progress, for the track had not freshened at all since we struck it many miles back. We topped out of a steep north slope onto a south exposure, where there was some grass, and we noted some tracks of loose horses.

"He ought to get him some meat here," I said.

"We'll get him quick if he does," Fisher replied and added, "maybe save the rest of the bunch."

There was no further need of discussing the point, for the hounds had come upon the carcass of a roan saddle horse killed two nights before with a big meal eaten out of the loins. Great heaps of pine needles and grass had been raked up against the horse but it could not be covered all over. The track leaving there improved a lot but the lion had not been back last night. The hounds wasted little time at the carcass of the horse, but were off at once at a much better pace, heading back up country in full cry. We rode to them, hopeful they might jump their quarry soon, but that was not to be. On and on they went, fast on the shady slopes, much slower on the south exposures. The big old male lion was wandering here and there, making lots of scrapes, but headed nowhere in particular.

Once, on a steep, slick, north exposure above some cliffs, the dogs speeded up and we were riding fast to keep up when we were confronted with a big pine log lying up and down the hill. Nig jumped it without hesitation but, despite being sharp shod, almost fell when he landed on the icy hillside. As he regained his footing and started on, I turned in the saddle and yelled a warning to Fisher, but Old Turk was already clearing the log in a long, high jump. When he landed, his feet slipped and he fell flat. Miraculously, Fisher threw himself clear and, most fortunately, held on to the bridle reins. Turk floundered around trying to get up and started slipping slowly down the steep hill toward the brink of the cliff below. Quick as a flash, Fisher wrapped the bridle reins around the base of a little fir tree to stop the sliding horse.

"Whoa, Turk, easy boy, whoa, Turk, whoa," Fisher spoke soothingly to quiet the horse, then called to me, "Bring your saddle rope quick; whoa, Turk, whoa, now Turk."

As Turk quit struggling, I tied one end of the rope to the saddle horn and took a couple of wraps around a tree a few feet up the hill. Now he was secure and could not slip downhill any farther, but how to get him up on his feet again was the problem. While Fisher held the rope tight, he had me grab Turk's tail and pull him around so that he lay up and down, instead of across the hill. We let Turk rest a minute, patting and quieting him, then gently urged him to get up; at first he wouldn't even try in that awkward position. Finally, after a lot of coaxing and lifting to help straighten him up, he put his front feet out and got his forequarters up. He would have gone over backwards down the steep hill except for the rope anchoring the saddle to the tree. As he struggled and floundered, Fisher gave a little slack in the rope and he got up on his hind feet, also. Thus, he stood quivering a moment, then we cautiously led him out of that perilous predicament. I shudder to think what might have happened to both horse and rider had Fisher been less agile and quick thinking.

By the time we got going again the hounds were out of hearing and, disregarding the warning of the recent rugged experience, we rode as fast and recklessly as ever to catch up. We soon heard the hounds again in the box canyon below. Thinking they would go out on the other side, we crossed the rough canyon above the box and rode our sweat-lathered horses as fast as they could go along the rocky south exposure to try to intercept them and, perhaps, get a shot at the fleeing lion. Instead, they went back out the other way over the ridge and out of hearing. We began looking for a place to cross, when suddenly the pack, in full, excited cry, came within hearing again and headed down the hill right toward us as we watched from the opposite slope.

Soon they had come down through a break in the cliffs into the rugged canyon below and went up it baying as if they were right on the fleeing lion's tail. No sooner had we started that way than here they came back down the canyon, hell bent, making the canyon reverberate with their frantic baying and barking. Ever since they had jumped the old fellow way back where Fisher's horse fell, he had been ducking, dodging, circling, and doubling back on his track, trying desperately to get away and refusing to take refuge in a tree.

When he came back down the canyon to a point directly below us, he turned and started back up the opposite rough canyon wall. Fisher got a glimpse of him through the brush and trees some two hundred yards away. I didn't see him but the hounds were right on his tail talking business to him in no uncertain terms. Halfway up out of the canyon, he couldn't take it any longer and climbed a big limber pine tree. Completely exhausted from the long run ahead of the dogs, he spread himself out on some branches not more than twenty feet off the ground. The big tree was in a little opening on the hillside and we could see the huge old lion in it and the dogs frantically barking "treed" below him.

It was nearly four hundred yards across to our quarry, entirely too far to risk making a clean kill. The opposite canyon wall was much too rocky, steep, and slick to ride up, so I got rid of my chaps and spurs, pulled my rifle from the scabbard and set out afoot to make the trip, first down into the canyon and then to struggle up out of it to within shooting range. Fisher stayed with the horses to watch the lion and keep me advised of anything that might happen. It was a tough climb and I took it slowly because I didn't want to be badly out of breath should I have to make a quick shot. There were patches of crusted snow on the hillside where the hounds had gone up and I noticed it was streaked with red from their feet, cut and bleeding from the long, hard chase over frozen ground, crusted snow, and sharp rocks.

I tried to stay behind a screen of trees and bushes lest the sly old lion see me and jump out to try again to get away. Of a sudden, while still a hundred yards below the tree, Fisher called out, "Shoot quick, he is going to jump." I stepped out from behind some fir saplings just in time to see him turning around on his perch to face the slope ready to leap to it. I pulled up my rifle, and, in all haste, tried to get a bead on a vital spot and squeezed the trigger, very doubtful that it would be a clean kill, if, indeed, he would be hit at all.

Great was my satisfaction, and I know my partner's was even greater, when the big, tawny, long-tailed cat sank down on the branches, quivered briefly, then slid off backwards, stone-dead. My shot was more luck than skill. The bullet entered the lower left flank, ranged forward and upward through the lungs and out near the top of the opposite shoulder. The hounds, though near exhaustion from the grueling chase, wooled the carcass around in post mortem revenge and caused it to slip and slide down to where I was, and it was an easy matter to slide and tumble it on down into the canyon. There we hastily skinned the lion and, truly, he was a big rugged old fellow, with teeth well worn, and sides of a grayish color, clearly showing advanced age. We sliced strips of meat from the hams and fed the tired and hungry hounds.

It was sundown when, with the big soft skin tied on back of my saddle, we started down the canyon, hoping to get out of the very rough country before dark. After a little while we looked back to see if the three efficient, persistent and faithful hounds were coming. Ed and Drum were at our horses' heels, but little Fannie, limping along the dim trail, had dropped back quite a distance. We waited until she caught up, then Fisher took little, sore-footed Fannie in his arms and carried her on his horse all the way down to the Pecos River and up the long weary miles to the Arnold Ranch. We had been forty hours with nothing but potatoes to eat and were famished, but too tired to eat much, and soon turned in to spend what was left of the night there.

The two-week, thrill-packed lion hunt was over and we had four of the big male horse- and deer-killers to our credit, but not a sign of a female or young lion had we seen. In the two weeks, we had experienced the gratifying excitement, thrills, grueling work, hardships, and satisfaction which one may expect in many varying forms on any really good lion hunt.

While the Pecos high country in the region of Beatty's Cabin has never been a good lion country, and few have been taken there, the somewhat lower mountain areas forming its perimeter have been the scene of many a tine, soul-satisfying chase on the trail of his honor, *Felis concolor hippolestes.*

8
extirpation and restoration of elk

In his remarkable and fascinating book titled, "A Sand County Almanac," my dear friend, eminent naturalist, conservationist, and author, Aldo Leopold, who died in 1948, lament-ingly states, "In 1866 the last native Wisconsin elk was killed." It was about a quarter of a century later when the last native elk of the once plentiful bands that roamed the Pecos high country met a similar ruthless fate. The exact date is not known, but it is of little consequence whether it happened in 1888 or five years earlier or later. *The tragedy is that the last elk was killed.*

Don Juan Pendaries was an old Frenchman who settled in the Rociada Valley, just across the ridge from our place on Sapello Creek in the late i86o's. When I was a small boy, he told me about elk coming into his big hay meadows when he first came there. He said he had seen bands of a hundred or more in the late evenings and early mornings, grazing in his meadows when the snow lay deep in the high country. Each year their numbers became less and less, as the settlers and prospectors raided the herds more and more for their winter's meat.

Just after I had written the paragraph above, to check my memory I called up Don Juan Pendaries' daughter, Mrs. Marguerite P. Baca, former New.Mexico secretary of state, and she said she, too, remembered very well her father telling about how the elk once habitually fed in his hay meadows.

In 1881, naturalist L. L. Dyche reported that he saw a fine bull elk on Beaver Creek, east of the upper Pecos country and three miles south of our place on Sapello Creek, but did not get a shot at it. That, perhaps, is the last written record of a native elk being seen in the region. A year later, Dyche wanted very badly to obtain a specimen or two for the University of Kansas Museum but found none in the upper Pecos area. He heard that some were ranging at the head of Santa Barbara Creek and Rio de la Casa and the ridges north of the Pecos toward Jicarita Peak. He made an extended trip into those areas from his "Bear Trail" Camp on Rito del Oso, but, unfortunately, failed to find any.

In 1883, E. W. Nelson, who later became chief of the U. S. Biological Survey, spent several months in the upper Pecos country; and, although it is reported that he heard of elk in the area, he saw none. It was mentioned in a previous chapter that my brother Charlie, in 1896, dug the fairly well preserved antlers of a big bull elk out of a pile of driftwood, sand, and debris at the mouth of Rito de los Esteros. For years after that whenever we went into the mountains, we were always looking for elk tracks or droppings as evidence that a few of these fine game animals had escaped, but alas! we looked, and looked in vain, for by that time they were all gone. The occasional finding of pieces of old decaying antlers served to intensify our regrets that they had been wiped out, but did not raise our hopes that any had survived.

When roaming through this vast, remote mountain mass with its dense alpine forests, aspen thickets, precipitous slopes and deep, meandering canyons, one wonders how an animal as astute and resourceful as an elk is when persistently hunted, could be completely wiped out. Truly, on their summer range it would be difficult to hunt them down to the last animal; some wild remnants would be bound to escape. But, in winter, elk became more vulnerable for it was their habit to congregate into herds and drift out into the lower, more open and accessible, country to winter, even as the Yellowstone herds do today. Trappers, settlers, miners, and market hunters were alert and quick to take advantage of this traditional migration. Unfortunately, the elk's hereditary habits, like those of many other wild animals, are not easily changed even in the face of powder and lead.

Then, too, in their natural state, elk were preyed upon to a considerable extent, in summer, by grizzly bear. Thus beset by their natural control predator in summer and in winter by a far more destructive, artificial predator—man, with his powder, lead, and insatiable lust to kill—these noble game animals were unable to withstand the double pressure and gave up the ghost. The sequel, equally tragic, is that when the herds of elk were gone and cattle put on the summer range in their place, grizzly bear naturally took to killing the cattle to such an extent that, a few years later, to make the wilderness safe for cows, nature's crowning wildlife achievement, the mighty grizzly was likewise extinguished.

The Rocky Mountain bighorn sheep, also, were indigenous to this and other areas of the state but their meat was considered the best of all wild meat and, hence, they were sought after like select items on a bargain counter. Ruxton, an English naturalist who passed this way in 1846, reported that at Questa, a hundred miles north of Santa Fe, he was fed on mountain sheep meat by his overnight hosts and remarked that it was considered a delicacy and preferred above other wild meats.

In 1873, Coues and Yarrow reported sheep were plentiful in the mountains east of Santa Fe (the upper Pecos) but they were to disappear rapidly after that. Tom Stewart told me many times that the last mountain sheep killed in the area was taken by Jim Bullock at the base of Santa Fe Baldy, near Lake Kather-ine? In 1902; however, naturalist Vernon Bailey reports in his *Mammals of New Mexico* that he saw unmistakable tracks of mountain sheep in the Truchas Peaks area in 1903. There is no positive record that a native sheep has been seen in the area since that time.

It is most probable that rifles were not the sole cause of the depletion of these denizens of the high, timber-line area. When domestic sheep were brought into the high country to graze for brief summer periods, they were often infected with scabies and, perhaps, other communicable diseases or parasites which could easily be transmitted to the bighorns. Domestic sheep could be cured of scabies by forcing them to swim through vats of Black Leaf 40 solution, but Nature provided no such method of treatment for the wild bighorns, and they would be defenseless against the ravages of parasitic infections or diseases new to them, just as the Indians were against smallpox, first brought to them by the white man.

Whatever the cause, with the untimely passing of these spectacular creatures, the jagged crags and templed peaks very definitely lost something of their hereditary charm and glory. On timber-line ridges and in the coves, alpine clover each year sends up its velvety, gray-green leaves and pink-white blossoms in supplication for the return of God's free wild creatures who once fattened upon its succulence. But none return to eat it. The brows of the high, grassy hills, furrowed and wrinkled by unnatural gullies, frown disapprovingly upon the substitution of herds of domestic woollies for the little bands of wild bighorns that once scanned the glorious landscape from their crests. Restoration is past due.

One effort was made, in 1933, by the State Department of Game and Fish to re-establish bighorns in the Pecos high country. Six animals, two bucks and four ewes, were obtained through the courtesy of the Canadian National Park Service from Banff, Alberta, Canada, and released at the west base of the range. A year later the two rams were seen by Forest Ranger J. W. Johnson at the head of the Pecos on the Santa Barbara Divide, but they have not been heard of since and it must be presumed they met the same fate as their native predecessors. With the material reduction of the number of domestic sheep permitted to summer graze this extremely high vulnerable area and the elimination of the dread scabies from the herds, there is now a good possibility that the Rocky Mountain bighorns might yet be restored to their hereditary range. God speed the day!

The story of the interesting and valuable little dam-building fur bearers is much like that of the Rocky Mountain sheep and the elk. The pioneer mountain men of the West who diligently sought after beavers for their valuable fur, apparently never heard of beaver trapping management to provide a sustained annual yield. They were greedy for the day's selfish gain and looked to the future not at all. While there was evidence throughout the Pecos high country fifty years ago that beavers had once made it their home, there was only one place that I knew of where the signs of these expert and industrious little engineers were at all recent. That was at the site of a series of their old dams in the deep canyon of the Pecos, two miles below Beatty's Cabin. Just how long it had been since a colony of beavers lived and labored there one could not say, but when I was first at the old dams, in about 1902, the workings looked as though they had been deserted for ten or fifteen years, maybe more. There is little doubt that this spot in the willowy, narrow meadow, between two segments of the box canyon, was the tragic scene of their last stand in the Pecos watershed. Like many ghost towns throughout the mountains of the West, where ambitious miners once lived, loved, and worked, so was this also a ghost town as real as the others.

The beavers on the head of the Rio de la Casa, which lies over the high, near-timber-line divide to the northeast of the head of the Pecos, fortunately were not all trapped out, although they were reduced to minimum numbers for years. Then, when better protection came in the 1920's, the number of colonies began to increase and there were some fine dams to be found in the Rincón Bonito and other forks of the Rio de la

Casa. Then a most interesting incident occurred. By tracing the signs, in 1932, it was very easy to see what had happened.

In the spring of 1930, a pair of beavers left their well-established home in Rincón Bonito and, on their stubby, short legs, waddled their way up to the top of the timber-line divide and down into the headwaters of the Pecos. Once on the stream, they began exploring the possibility of setting up housekeeping in likely spots. Where they first hit the stream, they cut a few willows and started to build a little dam, then abandoned it, and went on down to the big willow meadows above the falls. Willows were cut here and there along the stream and another little dam had been started but was soon abandoned like the first one.

The next sign was below the falls where an aspen six inches through had been cut and the limbs trimmed off of it. On down the stream, they left their sign, an aspen cut here, a peeled willow stick there. Just above Beatty's Cabin, another feeble start on a dam had been made, but, evidently, either the site or the available material was not satisfactory and they set out downstream again, leaving a little sign here and there as they went. At last, they passed through the first box canyon and on to the site of the old dams. There they set to work in earnest and soon had some new dams built below the springs in the marshes at the side of the creek, where the old dams had been. There, in a place to their liking, they have nourished and rehabilitated the area and chased the ghosts away.

Beaver migrations are not uncommon but it is most interesting to speculate on the reason why this particular pair left its happy home, crossed a high mountain range, and traveled eight miles downstream, passing up many suitable home sites, until they reached the spot where their predecessors had made their last stand, many decades before. What instinct prompted them to seek a new home by going over a high mountain range? Why did they refuse to settle down until they reached the site of the last habitation? Perhaps they were simply the counterpart of certain bipeds of the covered wagon days.

Inspired by this remarkable effort at recolonization, the State Department of Game and Fish set to work and within a few years, had trapped beavers from areas of plenty elsewhere and moved them, mostly in pack boxes on horseback or mule-back, into every suitable place in the whole upper Pecos area. Now beaver workings, perhaps, are again beginning to resemble the scene as it appeared in the days of Kit Carson.

The extirpation of elk and Rocky Mountain bighorn sheep, and the reduction of many other species of wildlife in New Mexico to pitifully small and scattered remnants of their former bountiful numbers, has made the work of the State Department of Game and Fish for the last forty years largely that of restoration. How utterly foolish and short-sighted it was to kill off the last of the elk and the mountain sheep, for no sooner were they gone than we found that we wanted and needed them back. The grizzly is sorely missed, too, although there is doubt that his cattle-killing propensities will ever permit his restoration. Restoration, it should be remembered, is costly and takes a lot more time than destruction does, whether it be animals, plants, or watersheds.

When the New Mexico Department of Game and Fish was created, in 1903, its finances were almost nil, barely enough to employ a state game warden and an office clerk. Yet, from the outset, Warden Page B. Otero, pioneer wildlife conservationist that he was, understood the desirability for restoration of that which had been lost, as well as the crying need for protection of what was left of the state's wildlife resources. But it was not until a dozen years and several wardens later that the restoration of elk to the Pecos high country was undertaken.

Despite the continued handicap of meager funds, in 1914, Warden Trinidad C. de Baca admirably determined to re-establish elk in the area. W. H. Bartlett, wealthy owner of the famed Vermejo Park country, had imported elk in 1908 and gotten them started there. De Baca's predecessor, Thomas P. Gable, had imported a few for the Webster Ranch, at Cimarron, the Poke Smith Ranch, near Raton, and a few others for the Gallinas area, so De Baca decided to restore them to the Pecos high country, funds or no funds. He persuaded the Secretary of the Interior through the National Park Service to donate two carloads of Yellowstone Park elk for the purpose. (They had to be shipped by railway car then, whereas now they are shipped by truck.) The transportation would be a big item so he induced the Atchison, Topeka and Santa Fe Railway Company to haul them much of the way free of charge, and the magnanimous co-operation of the company was a big help. He was then all set to get his elk, in December, 1914.

Then he realized that it would be unwise to release the elk to shift for themselves through the long snowy winter on range entirely new to them and, no doubt, quite different from that to which they were accustomed. Hurriedly, he persuaded the owners of Valley Ranch, a guest ranch on the Pecos River eighteen miles from the edge of the prospective elk range, to build a high, stout corral to hold them in, where they could be fed until spring. The project, with all concerned co-operating, was carried out according to plan. Fifty head of elk were shipped, but only forty survived the ordeal of shipping and confinement in the feed lot until spring. The survivors consisted of ten bulls and thirty cows. In the feed lot, the elk lost flesh and became downright poor and weak, and there was much criticism of the way they were being fed, or, rather, not being fed. It was later found that the untold numbers of ticks with which they were infested was the real cause of their emaciated condition.

Came April, 1915, and time for the release, but how to get them to their summer range, eighteen miles away, was the problem. They would have to be driven, for in those days there were no facilities for trucking them. None of the local people had ever driven an elk anywhere and nobody knew just how to go about it and what the elks' reaction would be when released. There is an old saying in ranch country that a good cowboy can do anything, so a dozen men, who could qualify as good mountain cowboys, were recruited. They included my two brothers-in-law, Charles and Emery Arnold, Forest Ranger C. E. Moore, now supervisor of the Lincoln National Forest, Ranger Harry Viles, Seborn Gray, Fermin Cortez, Joe Baca, and others.

The men were well mounted and ready for anything, and really expecting the elk to scatter to the four winds when the corral gate was opened and the elk came out, for better or for worse. At once two or three of the bulls, which were stronger than the cows, made a break for the timber and the men expected the herd to follow, but they headed up the road peacefully instead. The obstreperous bulls soon saw that the others were not following so they turned and trotted back to join the herd. All the way up the canyon, first one bull and then another would break away from the herd but every time they would turn and come back when they saw the others were not following.

On the way up the Pecos River several cows died. Mr. Moore recently said, "All the losses were poor cows, and when they became exhausted, they braced their feet, turned their heads to one side and twisted their under jaws sideways. That spelled 'curtains' for them and they could not be moved, but soon laid down and none of them ever got up again." The drive was slow, and by nightfall they were only a little over half way. There they were fed and held in a field overnight. It was near the settlement of El Macho, and there was plenty of volunteer help to night-herd the animals. Next morning early they were lined out again. They followed the canyon to the junction of the Pecos and Mora rivers, where they were turned up the ridge to the south side of Grass Mountain and left to shift for themselves.

Charles Arnold reports that he checked the herd the next day and the animals seemed to be content, but with only thirty-seven head left.

Elk were back on their home range. No longer would we look in vain for tracks and droppings. No longer would our findings consist of scraps of old decayed antlers. Within a year there would be ten sets of freshly shed antlers somewhere in the woods. No longer need we listen without hope of reward for the thrilling bugle of bulls, come mating season. The temporary loss of a part of their fascination and charm would be restored to the forests and parks. But the Pecos high country is large, and the meager thirty-seven head of elk, released on the edge of the wilderness, had before them a big job of procreation and distribution to do before restoration would be complete. While the band of elk was released on the south slopes of Grass Mountain from whence it was expected they would drift north into the Hamilton Mesa and Beatty's Cabin region, they had a different idea. Often wild animals and birds, when released on new range which, to the best qualified observer, appears to be ideal for them, will drift off to some other, apparently less desirable, area to establish their new home. These elk, while apparently content at first on Grass Mountain, within the year drifted eight miles south across the Mora River at the mouth of Bear Creek and Willow Creek and established their home base around Jack's Mesa at the head of Chaparrito Creek, on the H. S. Arnold Ranch, where they were well protected, salted and fed with the cattle in winter.

For several years the newly-established elk were to be found only on Cow Creek and its tributaries, Chaparrito, Soldier, Sheep, and Elk creeks. Then they moved southward into Bull Creek and Rito Del Osha and northward into Willow Creek and Bear Creek. In 1922, Forest Ranger M. M. Bruhl and I saw three head on the Lone Tree Mesa, six miles east of the Pecos Divide. They did not stick well on that side of the mountain, however, and have, for some unexplainable reason, never became plentiful there. The next year, while looking after my cattle, (I was ranching from 1919 to 1930) I ran onto a bunch of about twenty head of cows and heifers in an old burn at the head of Bear Creek. They bristled up the hair on their necks and withers and almost ran over me, for I had gotten between them and their young calves, which they had parked here and there among the logs. Then the little spotted fellows responded to the half-grunting, half-bleating noise their mothers were making, got up, and followed them to cover of the spruce forest bordering the old burn.

After that, their sign was seen in the Valle Medio, then the Rito Los Esteros, Hamilton Mesa, and Valdez Creek. Gradually they were progressing toward the Beatty's Cabin area and the real Pecos high country surrounding it, which we anticipated would, and which in reality has, become the heart of the elk range. It was probably in 1929 or 1930 when they first crossed the main Pecos River, but they liked it there when they did cross and multiplied and scattered on to the north and west. Both George Viles and L. W. Simmons noted a rapid build-up in the Beatty's Cabin area in the early 1930's.

Meanwhile, the herd was suffering some severe reverses lower down. The American Metal Company had begun operating the big mines at the mouth of Willow Creek, in 1926, with about six hundred men employed. Many of these were drifters with no interest in the local resources of the country. Others were people who lived on the east and north side of the mountains who traveled horseback about once a month through the mountains going to or from their jobs. A lot of them, and some of the local people as well, developed a taste for elk meat, despite the fact that there was no open season. The Game Department did not have sufficient funds to cope fully with this lawless destruction of the much-prized game, and the increase was greatly retarded in the Willow Creek, Bear Creek, Valle Medio, and Cow Creek country until the mines were closed, in 1939.

During my trips to Beatty's Cabin country in 1931, 1932, and 1933, fifteen years after the release had been made, much sign and, occasionally, a small band of elk were observed. What a warm satisfaction it was to know that restitution for the shame of extermination had at last been made. What a gratifying thrill it was when, on the trail five miles above Beatty's Cabin, I found an unusually fine matched set of freshly shed antlers. Big and cumbersome as they were, I carried them all the way back and still have them in my garage today. It was a fitting reward for the countless times, in earlier years, that I had looked in vain for tracks, droppings, or solid antlers.

In Beatty's Parks tall bunch grass tickles elk bellies as of old, and nods its drooping heads approvingly with every passing breeze. Saplings proudly display long white blazes where fine bulls have cleaned their horns of velvet. Larger aspens exhibit little orange-colored scars where bits of bark have been chiseled out during a snowstorm for food, with an upward stroke of elk front teeth. Oblong patches of flattened grass in secluded glades proclaim that a band of elk have recently bedded there. The many little piles of black wapiti "marbles," counterpart of the big, thick bovine "pancakes," on blue grass slopes assure one he has found a favored feeding ground.

Indeed, with the return of elk, the Pecos high country has won back much of its lost enchantment so that men and women, oppressed and harassed by the claustrophobia of high-tension living, may attain fuller release and more intensively enjoy the charms and freedom of the wilderness.

9

climbing
the peaks

The upper Pecos basin is surrounded by a high, horseshoe-shaped divide all the way from Barrillas Peak, on the east, to Glorieta Baldy, on the west, a distance of nearly a hundred miles. For the most part, this divide is over eleven thousand feet in elevation. With the lone exception of Elk Mountain, the peaks and hogbacks rising above timber line are on the north and west sides. The dozens of canyons heading against the precipitous outside curve of the horseshoe are as rugged and picturesque as any within the basin, and their headwaters are included in the area referred to as the Pecos high country.

The triple peaks called "Truchas" dominate the northwest curve of the horseshoe, and are sufficiently high and rugged to challenge the endurance and skill of those seeking the thrills and adventures of mountain climbing above timber line. Of the three peaks, South Truchas is the highest, poking its bald top up to 13,110 feet. Middle and North Truchas are almost as high, while the north peak is the most rugged of the three. While many people have climbed these and other peaks of the region, none have done so as often and gotten so much pleasure out of it and so many fine scenic pictures as Harold Walter, of whom we shall hear more later on.

My first trip to the cloud-scraping top was in 1903, when, at the age of sixteen, I was employed as a guide for an engineer named Powers. His mission was to determine whether or not it was possible to make a transmountain diversion of water from the heads of Mora and Valdez creeks to the east side of the range, by ditching it around the mountain to a slight gap in the main range.

We made the trip on horseback from our ranch on Sapello Creek, leading an old lop-eared burro carrying our light camp outfit. Base camp was made in a big, beautiful meadow near the head of the Mora River. By the end of the third day, Mr. Powers had found out that, since water won't run uphill, the proposed diversion was out of the question. But we had come prepared to stay ten days so decided to make the alluring trip to the top of Truchas Peaks. We chose to follow around the high, trailless divide at the head of the Pecos and found it a highly scenic route with continuous magnificent views to right and left as well as straight ahead. We pitched camp at sundown at a cold little spring just below timber line, at the head of Rito del Padre. I carried a .22 rifle and shot the heads off some half-grown grouse as we came along, for camp meat, and we found them even more delicious than the fine trout we had feasted upon at the previous camp.

Big, round Cerro Chimayosos towered above us back of camp and next morning we rode to its 12,944-foot crest; but that wasn't enough for us, so we worked our way down the steep, rocky slope to the deep saddle that lies between this peak and the North Truchas. We rode up the east shoulder of Truchas Peak to timber line, where we tied our horses to some low, flat-topped spruce trees. From there on, we made the long roundabout climb up the jagged peak afoot. The extreme altitude of over 13,000 feet and the exertion affected Powers strangely. By the time we got to the top, he became as a drunken man, staggering about, and laughing and talking nonsensically. He didn't seem to realize that anything was wrong or that he was acting at all abnormally. I was scared stiff lest he have heart failure or go completely insane here on the rugged mountaintop miles and miles from anywhere.

We didn't take much time to look, but I well remember the view from the top of the peak was one of surpassing magnificence. Most of the surrounding landscape was bathed in bright sunlight, while big, black thunder clouds had formed right over the peaks and we were in deep shadow. This situation seemed to clarify our view all the way from the foreground to the far distant horizons. We could see the lowering peaks of the Taos Mountains and, far beyond them, into Colorado to the north; to the east, the beautiful upper Pecos basin and the broad plains far beyond the Main Range; to the south were the irrigated valleys fifty miles below, and the plains and mesas a hundred miles farther on; and to the west, across the picturesque Rio Grande valley, were the sprawling Jemez Mountains, and a little farther north we could see into the San Juan Range and the valley of the Chama River.

It was a panorama never to be forgotten and one could have stood and gazed for hours, drinking in the grandeur, but that was not to be. Instead, Powers' continued unusual reaction to the altitude, coupled with the ominous aspect of the rapidly gathering thunder clouds, suggested that we better get the heck off of that peak as fast as we could. We scrambled down over rock slides and boulders and around cliffs, but the going was too rough to make much time despite our every effort to hurry.

By the time we reached the horses, Powers' flighty spell had pretty well passed, but the lightning was flashing and sizzling all around, much too close for comfort. We quickly mounted, and, as we started down, it began to rain. As if they had been punctured by the tops of the peaks, the clouds seemed to burst wide open and poured the water out. Much to our regret, we had inadvertently left our slickers in camp, and, for fear of being struck by lightning, dared not take shelter under a tree. We rode on down to the low saddle as fast as we could in the torrential downpour, which soon turned to fine hail, whitening the ground like a winter snowstorm. We kept to open areas as much as possible and got the worst soaking anybody ever got.

Within the hour, the fury of the storm had passed but by then we were so cold, wet, and miserable that we wondered whether we would ever get to camp or not. We had to walk and lead our horses most of the way to keep from freezing. At camp, we finally got a fire started and spent hours drying out.

The glimpse of the magnificent and colorful panorama from the towering crest of jagged North Truchas Peak was entirely too brief for fullest enjoyment, but was plenty long enough to make one want to go back. That I have done on several occasions but never again with a man who got drunk on thin air.

A few years later, my two adventuresome younger brothers, S. Omar and David Marion, and two young friends, made a trip from the ranch just to climb the Truchas. They were successful in reaching the rocky crest of all three peaks. They were just kids and had a lot of thrills and fun. Since S. Omar Barker is a professional author and story teller, let's have the tale from him first-hand:

The Magic Mountains

"To a couple of dream-headed, bean-hoeing buttons on the upper Sapello, 'Pecos' was always a magic name. We probably had never heard of its long, quick-sandy tail winding away to Texas, fabulous in cow country history for alkali and gun-smoky argument. To Marion and me the 'Pecos' meant an equally fabulous river of the wilderness, a magic Mecca of the mountains somewhere over beyond the Main Range, where, as soon as we got big enough, we might go camping with Pa or Charlie or Elliott, to see more sights and catch more big red-bellied trout than Carter had oats.

"I don't remember how old we were when we finally got to go, but I do remember vividly my first sight of the triple Truchas Peaks from Spring Mountain as they lifted snow-pintoed pyramids to awesome heights above the dark spruce timber below. To me they looked gosh-awful high, but Marion promptly said, 'Let's climb 'em!'

"One way or another, it was not until Marion was well into the tail-end of his teens with me two years behind that we finally got around to it. A couple of school friends, Carl Brorein (now President of the Peninsular Telephone Company at Tampa, Florida) and Alfred Livingston (now a professor of geology in California) went with us, and tame though it may seem in the telling, to us it was something of an adventure.

"Pa spared us a horse apiece to ride and one to pack. With camp 'extras' bulging our slicker rolls and Marion thumbing his little Fannie mare to make her buck and show off a little, we set out at sun-up one crisp July morning, camping that afternoon on the Mora Fork early enough to catch all the trout we could eat.

"We knew nothing about what few trails there were toward Truchas Peaks; thus, instead of intercepting the trail off Hamilton Mesa to Beatty's Cabin the next morning, we somehow skidded smack down into the Pecos Box and could find no way out on the other side. What we did find was some pools with more visible big trout than you could shake a stick at—only to discover that we had inadvertently left all our fishhooks at the Mora Fork camp. A hailstorm hit and, in putting on our slickers, we found some of their buttons were safety pins, which Marion promptly shaped into fishhooks, and with short willow poles, horse tail hair for lines, hellgrammites for bait, and a thunderstorm for weather, we horsed out half a dozen 12-inch natives in a few minutes of the most exciting fishing I ever enjoyed.

"Getting the horses back up the steep, loggy, thick-timbered, rock-ribbed, moss-slippery, soaking-wet slope to find the trail we had missed,

84

used up the rest of the day. Wet and weary, we made camp about dark at Beatty's Cabin—which we should have reached by noon.

"Next morning we headed out up the steep hill back of Beatty's with Marion in the lead. He claimed he knew which way the Peaks were—and he did. The only trouble was that there seemed to be a few million spruces, a few thousand log-falls, and a few hundred boggy marshes in the way. Hour after hour we put our poor ponies over and through the tangled mess, bogged them to their bellies in primrose-scented marshes, wind-busted them up steep, rocky benches, to make camp finally in a drizzly twilight at the edge of a green, soggy meadow with fog-shrouded glimpses of the snow-streaked Peaks looming close above us—'not much farther away,' as Marion said, 'than Ol' Man Butler could spit.'

"Low clouds completely claimed the peaks the next morning and a steady rain resolved us to rest our tree-bumped knees in camp and wait for more wishful weather. But it is part of the magic of the high Pecos country that the most miserable rain can break off abruptly into starlight or sun, and the next morning found us tying up our horses in dazzling sunlight beside a crystal lake half a mile above camp, ready, at last, to sure 'nough climb the fabulous Truchas. To a rope-and-crampon mountain climber the easy ascent would have seemed a joke. To four-bug-eyed boys it was wonderful.

"Far above us three big bucks high-tailed it along the sag between the two north peaks, their great sprangly velvet-covered antlers etched sharp against a deep blue sky. They looked so big we thought they must be unknown left-overs of the Pecos elk herd then supposed to be extinct. Probably they weren't, but we got a thrill out of thinking so.

"We topped out on the sag where they had run, rimmed our way to the top of the north peak, then back across the sag to the middle one and finally to the rocky tip of the south peak, kingpin of them all. We didn't care whether this was the highest point in New Mexico or not. To us it was plainly the top of the world, a magnificent world of magic mountains velveted with dark spruces and bright aspen, topped out with raw rock beribboned with snowdrifts, and jeweled here and there with God's little looking-glasses that men call mountain lakes. From far off the Truchas Peaks had seemed a fabulous Carcassone, but unlike Carcassone, they were even more fabulous with sharp beauty, once attained.

"Maybe I'm nuts, but I think every boy should sometime climb a few mountain peaks—and preferably the Truchas! Pretty good stuff for a girl, too, especially if she is your own mountain-loving wife!

"Years later, Elsa and I climbed these proud pinnacles of the Pecos together from a snug camp in a mariposa flowered, bunch grass park on the North Rito Azul. Although this time we rode in by a reasonably open trail up the trouty Chimayosos and North Azul instead of slambanging through timber, log-tangle, and bog, and even rode a fair distance up the South Peak's shoulder before taking it afoot, we found it still the top of the world—a wonder world, well worth the short winded climb it takes to get there."

A Risky Winter Climb

While many people have climbed the Truchas Peaks, as far as I have been able to determine only one trip was ever made in the dead of winter. Credit for that unusual and perilous adventure is due Forest Ranger J. W. Johnson, now retired, and D. A. Shoemaker, Forest Service Inspector of Grazing, now deceased. From Mr. Shoemaker's official report and a narrative report by Ranger Johnson, the following story of their most unusual, hazardous, and daring trip has been gleaned:

The object of the trip is stated to be, "To observe general winter conditions as to snowfall, domestic stock, game, etc., in an area where records are meager or lacking." Knowing the two men well, I'll bet they were secretly itching for the adventure and thrill of doing something no one else had ever done. On Marcn 5, 1928, the two left the Viles Ranch (Mountain View) at 1:00 P.M., on skis, for Beatty's Cabin. They led Johnson's good horse, Scott, pulling a seven-foot toboggan loaded with their bedrolls, provisions, and equipment. This method was used instead of packing the* horse because they doubted if the horse would be able to get all the way to Beatty's, and, in that case, they would pull the toboggan on in themselves and send the horse back.

The snow was wet in the afternoon sun and traveling on skis was heavy work, but they were fortunate to get the toboggan-pulling horse all the way through. They followed the Hamilton Mesa route, arriving at Beatty's at midnight, after eleven hours of tedious work, both horse and men pretty well fagged out. They put a warm blanket on the sweat-covered horse, fed him a *mortal* of oats and turned him out in the pasture, where, on the steep south exposure, he could paw down through the snow for some bunch grass. The men were too tired to get supper and, after nibbling a sandwich and sipping a cup of coffee, crawled into their warm sleeping bags to relax and rest their tired aching muscles.

The next day was mostly spent resting with but a short ski trip up the Rito del Padre to observe snow and other conditions. They found the snow in the bottom in the vicinity of Beatty's Cabin only about thirty inches deep. The winter had been one of exceedingly light snowfall and throughout the general area at relative elevations the snow was found to be only about half normal depth. Even so, game had, as is customary, drifted out to lower ranges.

At 1:30 A.M. on the third day, Johnson and Shoemaker, mounted on skis, with the full moon shining brightly, set out for the top of South Truchas Peak, seven miles away and 3,886 feet higher. The route was up through the lower Beatty Parks, then over an old, dim trail to the north side of Rito Cebadilloso. From there, they went up through aspen groves, then cork bark fir and Englemann spruce timber, and, finally, up through the steep bunch-grass parks, now deeply covered with snow, to the head of Cebadilloso Canyon.

The climb, so far, was trying enough, but to get up the last quarter mile to the divide before dropping into the South Azul was a terrific strain. Shoemaker says, "A few hundred feet could be negotiated in, no other way than on all fours, with knee, toe, and hand holds in the crusted snow necessary to progress and, indeed, to prevent losing valuable distance already gained." From there, traveling was easier past the head of the South and North Azul, following the base of Bordo Lajado, and, at last, topping out at the last gap in the main divide south of the peaks.

On top of the divide, they encountered a strong, cold west wind and much blowing snow, but on and on they went, determined to reach their bleak, sky-scraping objective. The patches of timber afforded some shelter from the wind; but, when they reached the last clump of trees, the outlook was pretty bleak. The crest of the sharp ridge leading up to the peak was bare, the snow having blown off and combed out on the east side to a depth of fifty feet or more. The skis were left at the last timber, and the slick, rocky climb to the top was made on foot, as they leaned heavily against the gale to prevent being blown off the knife-edged ridge.

At exactly 10:10 A.M., they reached the top, 13,110 feet above sea level, having labored hard for eight hours and forty minutes. On the sharp top of the peak they estimated the wind velocity at fifty miles per hour and the temperature away below zero. Quickly a few pictures were snapped. They wanted more but, to their dismay, found their fingers too numb with cold to reload the camera.

Suddenly, Johnson noticed Shoemaker's face was-turning white and he exclaimed, "Your face is freezing, let's get off of here."

"It does feel kind of numb."

"It's white, it's freezing; let's go, and you rub your face hard as we travel."

Johnson had a wool-lined cap that covered his face, except his eyes, but Shoemaker was not so well protected.

They were both mighty happy to get back to the first clump of timber, get on their skis again and head downhill. Ranger Johnson's narrative says, "We headed down toward the Valle Azul. I went down the precipitous slope with caution but Dave, being a good skier, went straight off and wide open. At the bottom, where the ground levels off, he did not make the turn and the hole in the snow that he made would have buried a small house. At last he got untangled, but so much snow had gotten inside his clothes that he began to chill and was in a bad way. I finally got a fire started by a big, dead spruce tree in a protected spot and, after a couple of hours by the fire, he was all right again. We went down the North Azul, then on down the main canyon, but the snow by then had become soft, making the going very tough. We reached Beatty's Cabin at 4:00 P.M. and I was the nearest to complete exhaustion that I had ever been in my whole life. Dave came in in better shape."

They had had enough of the Pecos high country in dead of winter, and, next day, laboriously made their way back to Viles' Ranch the same way they had come up.

Only a few deer and elk tracks were observed on Hamilton Mesa, none above Beatty's. Coyotes and snowshoe rabbits, who can travel on top of the snow, had made tracks even up to the face of the peak. Birds were scarce, only one blue grouse being flushed out of a spruce tree, and a few Canadian jays seen here and there.

Wildlife knows, perhaps better than man, that the Pecos high country is a good place to be out of during the bleak winter months.

Tragedy On Truchas

"Los Alamos women found dead at foot of Truchas Mountain" was the big headline in the *Santa Fe New Mexican,* on October 27, 1947. The women were Frances B. Krauss, 34, former WAC from Baltimore, Maryland, and Mildred Hartig, 25, of Evansville, Indiana. Both were secretaries employed by the Atomic Energy Commission, at Los Alamos, birthplace of the era-changing atomic bomb.

On the twenty-fifth of October, the two ladies drove from Los Alamos to the little town of Truchas, about twelve miles northwest of the North Truchas Peak. There they employed Sam Martin, a local farmer, as a guide to take them to the top of the peak. The three set out early on the following morning on horseback, to make the hazardous trip. The fall had been open, with little snow, but the high country, of course, was frozen hard and the lack of deep snow made the hillsides all the more slippery.

At the base of the North Peak, in an open spot just below timber line, they had to leave their horses. From there the long, slick, tedious climb was made on foot. They couldn't go straight up the west face of the rugged peak but had to make a big swing around through a gap and approach it from another way. They reached the top between 3:00 and 4:00 P.M., and, after feasting their eyes on the magnificent surrounding scenery, started the downward climb.

Suddenly, looking down across the barren, precipitous west slope from the gap between the South and Middle peaks, they saw their horses. It looked to be such a short distance compared to the roundabout way they had come up, that the women wanted to take the short cut to them. Martin, the guide, warned that the very steep, icy slope was too dangerous, and protested vigorously to any such attempt. Despite the warnings, Miss Krauss started anyway and had gone only a few steps when she fell and plummeted off down the rocky, frozen slope for several hundred feet. At last, her leg and head cut badly and bruised all over, she caught on a rock and stopped.

Tediously and with utmost caution, Miss Hartig and Martin worked their way down to where Miss Krauss lay, clinging to a small projecting rock to keep from tumbling on down the mountain. It was soon found that they could not move her without a rope. Miss Hartig insisted upon staying with her unfortunate companion while Martin made his laborious way back and around to the horses for a rope. He left them both clinging to the rock in a most perilous situation, realizing fully that if they relinquished their holds they would go sliding and tumbling for hundreds of feet on down into a rugged ravine at the base of the peak.

At the coroner's inquest, the guide testified that he went to the horses as fast as he could and got a rope and tried to get to the women again, but by then they had lost their holds and slid further down and he was unable to get to them. He could hear them crying for help, "Please do something, we are freezing to death."

Being unable to reach the poor, unfortunate women, in desperation, Martin started back for help. But when he reached the horses again, he could no longer see the poor creatures up on the perilous slope and, believing they had lost their holds and tumbled on down, he searched for them until midnight in the terribly rough area below. Unable to find them, he went for help.

Rescue parties from the Atomic Energy Commission, at Los Alamos, and State Police, from Santa Fe, reached the scene at eleven o'clock the following morning, but it was not until 8:30 P.M. that State Policeman Jerry Brunk and guide Sam Martin found the bruised and battered bodies in the bottom of a ravine several hundred feet below where they had last been seen clinging desperately to rocks on the barren, icy mountainside. All night was spent getting the bodies out of the ravine and then ten miles by horse to an ambulance waiting at the end of the road.

Thus, a planned week end of enjoyment in climbing the peaks ended in disaster and tragedy.

Loses Life In Quest Of Birds' Nest

Another death occurred in connection with climbing in the Pecos high country but it was not mountain climbing. In 1901, a young ornithologist, Frances G. Birtwell, on the edge of the Pecos Wilderness area, at Willis, now Cowles, was attempting to get the nest and eggs of a pair of Rocky Mountain evening grosbeaks from a limb high up in a yellow pine tree, when he lost his life.

The tree, situated in the back yard of the H. D. Winsor ranch house, was devoid of limbs up to about thirty feet and was leaning considerably. Birtwell had tied two lariat ropes together and used them in climbing the tree. He had one end of the long ropes tied around his body under the arms and the other end thrown over a big limb when he started down with the prized bird's nest and eggs. In some way, he lost his hold on the tree and, since it was leaning, he swung out away from it. He had hold of the other end of the rope and was letting himself down gradually when the big knot that joined the ropes together got caught in a crotch of the limb. As he hung some fifteen or twenty feet off the ground, he was neither able to climb back up the rope or to swing over to the tree again. The rope soon slipped up until it strangled him to death.

Tom Stewart, who was cooking at the Winsor ranch at the time, and others saw it all and frantically tried to find a way to save him, but without success. Stewart always felt very bad about this because there was a loaded shotgun in the house which might have been used to shoot the rope in two had they thought of it in time.

A Persistent Climber

Harold Walter, pictorial photographer and peak climber, tells the following interesting story of his peak-climbing adventures:

"The killing of a ten-point bull elk was the incentive for my first mountain climb in the Sangre de Cristo Mountains of northern New Mexico. Word had reached our office at Tererro that my friend, Ole Lee, had bagged a prize elk on the headwaters of Cow Creek. I was eager to photograph the trophy for this was the first elk hunt on the Pecos area. Next morning, the first Sunday in November, 1933, my wife, May, and I drove the Engineers' Ford truck up the very steep and narrow Willow Creek logging road. Below the Irwin Forks, we had considerable trouble getting the pick-up over a steep, muddy stretch of road; however, the compound low took us up to easier going.

"About a mile farther on, the road was covered with a sheet of ice; one false turn of the steering wheel would have plunged us down hundreds of feet to the bottom of the canyon. It was a relief when we ridged out at the timber-loading racks an hour later. Even though the snow was drifted deep in places, we pushed the Ford on to the hunters' camp, located on a point above the headwaters of Cow Creek. We found the camp deserted but we kindled a fire and had hot coffee. We could see wagon tracks on the timber road circling the upper end of Cow Creek, which told us the hunters had gone over to bring the elk to camp.

"Looking the country over through field glasses, we located a cairn on top of a high, bald mountain. We consulted the map we carried and found it to be Elk Mountain, elevation 11,661 feet, located on the south edge of the Wilderness area. On the spur of the moment, we decided to climb to the top of the peak. We started following the ridge to the left and immediately encountered snowdrifts which made walking difficult. Two and a half weary hours later, we came to a drift fence a quarter of a mile north of our objective. Following this fence to the right, we came out of the spruces to a shale-rock clearing directly under the summit. The wind was blowing a gale and had cleared the snow, so the climbing was less difficult the last hundred yards or so. Keeping in the shelter of the large rock cairn, which was about eight feet tall, we had our first breathtaking view of the rugged and majestic peaks back of the upper Pecos valley. We looked down on the deep canyon of Bear Creek to beautiful Valle en Medio, across the

91

Mora to Hamilton Mesa to the deep Pecos Canyon. Large, open parks formed a checkerboard in the timber under this long, snow-capped range. I told May that my objective next summer would be to climb each one of those peaks.

"Dropping off the southwest side of Elk Mountain, we came to the timber road, then went on to the hunters' camp. The party had not returned, so we decided to go on back to Tererro and take pictures later when the elk was brought to camp.

"My second mountain-climbing trip was made under more favorable climatic conditions since it was in the pleasant month of July, the first day, to be exact, in the year 1934. Dan Rogers and I had planned for weeks to climb to the top of rugged Santa Fe Baldy, west of Cowles. The day dawned bright and clear, and seven o'clock found us in the saddle, headed toward our goal. The trail was narrow and winding and steep and led us alternately through groves of tall, straight quaking aspens, grassy little parks where wild flowers grew in profusion, then dark green Englemann spruce trees, and, finally, past Stewart Lake, which glistened in the sunlight like a bright jewel. Saucy little squirrels scolded us as we rode along invading their forest domain. At one place, a blue grouse flew up unexpectedly in front of my horse and caused him to shy for an instant. Birds called to each other overhead and occasionally we caught the flash of a blue jay.

"After more than three hours, we arrived at a small corral a short distance from Lake Katherine. We unsaddled our horses —much to their relief, I am sure—and turned them loose in this enclosure. We then climbed the steep little trail that led us to the lake. What a sight it presented! It nestled there at the foot of Santa Fe Baldy like a blue sapphire, gleaming and dimpling in the bright sunshine. We took the trail along the right shoreline and followed it for about fifty feet. Then we set out straight up the hill. Why we chose that particular place where there was a sheer rock slide to climb, I don't know, but that is just what we did for about seven hundred feet, to a point overlooking the lake. From this point I took a picture of this azure-blue lake and Santa Fe Baldy. Perhaps you have seen the picture as it appeared on the cover of the *New Mexico Magazine* in August, 1936, and again in March, 1942.

"We circled the range which forms a horseshoe above the lake, with Santa Fe Baldy at the southeast. It was noon by the time we reached the rock cairn, and the invigorating air and grueling climb had given us ravenous appetites. So we sat down at the foot of the cairn, whose bench mark showed 12,629 feet, and ate our lunch and reveled in the scene that

Nature had spread before us. Last winter's snow still clung to the east ledge to a depth of fifteen feet, as if defying the summer sun to melt it. The blue sky formed a cloudless tent above us and we felt that no two had ever been more richly rewarded for a strenuous climb than we had been that day.

* * *

"My third mountain trip in New Mexico was made on July 4, 1934, accompanied by K. L. Wolford and Dan Rogers. We left Tererro at five o'clock and drove by car to the end of the road up Winsor Creek. At six-thirty we left the car for our objective, Lake Peak, eleven miles away by forest trail. We followed up the left of the creek to the ridge between Holy Ghost and Winsor Creek, past the Spirit Lake Fork to the divide at the head of the Nambe. Taking the trail to the left, we walked to timber line, where we followed the old telephone line to the remains of the rock shelter used as a fire outlook years ago on the summit of Penitente Peak. Dropping down the southwest side, we came to the trail at the saddle between the two peaks. From here the fairly steep trail zigzagged to the summit of Lake Peak.

"This Peak has an elevation of 12,408 feet, with perpendicular cliffs on three sides. We could see mountains in Colorado to the north. We could descry miles of the Rio Grande valley to the west. To the southwest we could look down on Santa Fe. Far below us on the Pecos it had begun to rain so we decided to have a quick lunch and get down off the mountain as soon as possible. By the time we came to the Nambe Divide, the rain was coming down in torrents. We still had seven miles to go to reach the car and we made good time all the way by alternately walking fast and dog trotting. We made the whole twenty-two mile trip in just nine hours of actual travel. Mr. Viles, at Cowles, was doubtful that we had made the climb but he was thoroughly convinced a few days later when I showed him pictures I had taken from the top of the peak.

* * *

"Later in the month the same year, Dan and I decided on another mountain trip—this time north to Pecos Baldy and the Truchas Peaks. We obtained horses at Cowles and were well on our way at one o'clock in the afternoon. Leaving the road above Los Pinos, we took the forest trail to the right. Circling the old Club House, we gradually climbed to the Round

Mountain corral. After resting the horses, we rode up to the left of Round Mountain to Jack's Creek. Following to the headwaters, we arrived at Pecos Baldy Lake at four-thirty in the afternoon. We staked our horses out to the left of the 11,742-foot high lake and started to climb the shale slide to the southeast of the granite peak. In an hour and forty-five minutes, we were at the large cairn on east Pecos Baldy, at an elevation of 12,500 feet. Directly north, the majestic Truchas Peaks reared their proud heads and fairly begged us to photograph them. We obliged gladly.

"We descended the northeast ridge to the upper end of the lake. By the time we reached the lake it was dark. We gathered wood, had supper and turned in for the night. Our upturned saddles proved to be too uncomfortable as beds and our slickers inadequate as cover, so by three-thirty we were ready to get up. We rekindled the fire, and, after we had gotten warm and had a delicious breakfast of bacon, eggs, and coffee, we were ready to go mountain climbing again. We saddled our horses and rode up over the rincon to the foot of South Truchas, a distance of about four miles. We tied the horses to a clump of dwarf juniper at timber line and started the climb about seven. We kept to the left of the ridge, encountering large boulders, which we managed to crawl over, and reached the summit of South Truchas about eight-thirty. Just as we arrived, a most beautiful thunder head formed over the North Peak. I immediately set up my camera and succeeded in shooting one of the best pictorial mountain scenes it has ever been my luck to get.

"While eating our lunch, the wind came up and black clouds formed. We knew this was the forerunner of a storm so we hurriedly gathered up our belongings and made a hasty descent. We reached the horses in less than an hour and headed for the lake, where we had left our sack of food and cooking utensils. We hadn't been on the horses fifteen minutes when all hell broke loose. Thunder crashed and lightning ripped across the skies. The clouds opened up! Hailstones half an inch in diameter beat down on us as we cringed in the saddles. The horses would not face it. There was no shelter, since the area was covered with shale rock with here and there a skeleton of a tree left by a forest fire of long ago, so we finally dismounted and led our horses more than two miles to the lake. The hail fell for over two hours. Our slickers were like sieves and our backs became sore and bruised from the pounding of the hailstones. We crawled, half-exhausted, under some foxtail pines and finally managed to get a fire going. We made some coffee, which revived our spirits immensely. It was a long, tiresome trip back to the ranch but, in spite of our exhaustion, we felt a glow of satisfaction in the fact that we had climbed the highest peak in the state— 13,300 feet. At that time that elevation was an accepted fact and the Truchas Peaks were considered to be the highest in New Mexico. Since then, I have had no small part in having the elevations rechecked and it has been found that South Truchas is actually 13,110 feet and that Wheeler Peak, in the Taos Mountains, is slightly higher.

"The first climb to the top of a towering, rock-ribbed peak no doubt gives one his greatest thrill, but there is always the desire to go back and do it again. Since my initiation, I have followed that urge and climbed these and other peaks many times and taken hundreds of pictures of magnificent alpine scenes."

Mrs. L. L. Dyche at age of 94, who honey-
mooned at Beatty's Cabin in 1884

Photo by Dalton-Brown,
Lawrence, Kan

Winter's snow linger to greet
may flowers in the high country

Photo by Harold D. Walter

Trail riders of the wilderness arriving
in Horse Thief meadows

Wilderness Trail Riders
pause for a last look at Truchas Peaks

Anglers at the edge
of Lost Bear Lake   *Photo by Harold D. Walter*

Pack trips are always satisfying,   *Photo by author*
Federal Judge Colin Neblett (now deceased) in lead

When early snows come elk linger
'till sun-up to graze in open parks

Triple Truchas Peaks tower
over Rito Chimayosos

Beavers restored to the Pecos high coutry are
busy cutting timber for new dams   *Photo by the author*

Penitente and Lake Peaks   *Photo by Harold D. Walter*
looking south from Santa Fe Baldy

On the trail burro-back to vacation
at Harvey's Ranch

From an old photo supplied by Mrs. Edna Fetterman

Photo by Harold D. Walter   Names carved on a huge spruce
tree at Beatty's Cabin in 1891

H. A. Harvey grandchildren arriving at Paradise Valley in pack boxes
From and old photo supplied by Dorothy Harvey

Lion hunters S. L. Fisher and Mrs. Fisher
with horses, hounds, and two lions

Snow clad North Truchas in nid-winter
taken from South Truchas

*From Camp Fires of
a Naturalist—D. Appleton & Co.*

Grizzly bear of the
Pecos high country

Beautiful, shimmering
Pecos Baldy Lake   *Photo by Harold D. Walter*

Baldy Lake regularly yields limits like this   *Photo by Harold D. Walter*
Left to right, Homer Pickens, Bob Ground, and Lee Wang

Outlaw cabin
at head of Pecos

Photo by Harold D. Walter

North Truchas Peak
taken from South Truchas

Heads of illegally taken elk and deer
found at outlaw cabin

Elk from Wyoming being held in corral
for release in the high country

Photo by Harold D. Walter

Wild turkey is royal game
Mrs. Elsa is lucky nimrod

Photo by S. Omar Barker

Photo by Harold D. Walter

Truchas Peaks and Cerro Chimayosos
looking north from Azul-Cebadilloso divide

Middle Truchas. Left center
where two girls fell to their death

Photo by Harold D. Walter

Photo by Homer C. Pickens

Mountain lion at bay
on cliff in rugged country

The author, 1932, with Puse
his famous lion-hunting Airedale

Photo by S. Omar Barker

Looking East from
Spring Mountain

Photo by Harold D. Walter

From Camp Fires of a Naturalist—
D. Appleton & Co.

George Beatty and his
"sure good bear knives"

The author views the high country from the spot
he first saw it as a ten-year-old boy in 1896

Beatty's Cabins, 1952. Left to right: Dr. Brubaker, Mrs. Brubaker,
Clarence Via, Mrs. Elliot Barker, and Isabelle Via   *Photo by the author*

Lake Katherine, unrivalled fishing   *Photo by Harold D. Walter*
and beauty spot of the high country

10

the big buck of the bear creek burns

It was near the end of the big game season in 1933 and Homer Pickens and I had not yet found time to go deer hunting. We felt we must go for some relaxation and rest, but we would have to hurry. There was snow in the Pecos high country and it was cold, but we decided to go there anyway. Naturally, I wanted to go to Beatty's Cabin, but my partner wanted to go to Valle Medio country, where he had seen some good bucks earlier in the fall. We would have to camp out, but our good cowboy friend, Dee Bibb, was camped there, where he had been on patrol ever since the season started and, if he could take it, we felt we could, too.

We packed out from Cowles and found Dee's camp in a small, sheltered park at the upper end of Valle Medio, which lies between Bear Creek and Rito de las Trampas. For a couple of days we hunted fairly close in and found plenty of game sign but the bucks were wild and hard to get sight of, for there had been much shooting earlier in the season. While huddled around the big, blazing campfire after supper one frosty night, we suddenly realized that there was but one day left until the season would be over. Tomorrow was our last chance.

"Where do you plan to hunt tomorrow, Homer?" I asked.

"Think I'll hunt north toward Rito de los Esteros," he said, and then as an afterthought, "unless you want to go there."

The old fellow swung to the right, keeping in the timber for a quarter mile. Then he slowly came out to the edge of an open, rocky knoll from where, well camouflaged, he could look back and see what the hunter was doing. The hunter tied his horse to a sapling and followed the tracks of the two bucks as if he expected them to stop there in the open area, as indeed they sometimes do when separated from a band. As the old, long-horned buck watched, he felt perfectly safe, but dared not go back to his beloved does for to do so might endanger them as well as himself.

The old buck watched the hunter as he moved forward slowly and carefully. He also watched the other bucks as they turned up the hill at right angles to their back tracks for a hundred yards or so, then came back parallel to them a short distance, where they took up vigil, peeking through the branches of some young fir trees. The cautious, red-capped hunter crunched along, watching straight ahead with rifle ready. When the hunter cautiously came along opposite the hiding place of the two bucks, they snorted contemptuously and bounded away out of sight. The hunter was so startled he nearly dropped his rifle and, before he could recover his senses, the bucks were safely out of sight. The nimrod brushed the snow off a log and sat down disgustedly. There he waited a long time wishing, without hope, that a buck would be silly enough to come within sight and range. Meanwhile, the long-horned buck moved to a more secluded spot and bedded down and waited patiently.

Finally, the hunter went back, got on his horse, and followed the big old buck's tracks across the burn and into the timber. The wise old fellow could hear the hunter coming toward him and, to fool him, got up and walked briskly on around the hillside for a little way, then circled in a trot up the hill, and then back to a spot from which he could see his bed without being seen. When the hunter came to the bed, he dismounted and looked longingly in the direction the buck had gone when he left the spot. At that instant Old Long Horns, from his vantage point up the hill, blew him a good-by, whistling snort, and bounded away through the timber. He ran a couple of hundred yards up the steep hill, and then stopped to listen. The horse made so much noise clambering over rocks and breaking dead limbs as he climbed the hill, that the buck could tell just where the hunter was at all times. The buck walked to the left, around the hillside for a short distance, then turned back down the hill to his own tracks and those of the horse, which he followed back to his old bed. From there, he continued on in the horse tracks up the hill when he heard the hunter coming along. Who was chasing whom, anyway?

As the buck went around the circle for the second time, often stepping right in the horse's tracks, he could hear the noisy hunter and kept well ahead of him. Then, as he approached his old bed, the noise stopped and he felt sure his tormentor had abandoned the chase. To verify that, the old fellow started on to his original lookout point, to watch for the hunter to see if he crossed the burn.

Suddenly he froze in his tracks. There at his old bed, through the trees, he could indistinctly see the hunter's black horse. The hunter had left his horse there, and had followed on afoot, very noisily for awhile, to make the buck think he was still horseback. Then he had become quiet to make the buck think he had given up the chase.

Now the old buck listened intently, but no sound came to him. He sniffed the air repeatedly, but it was so pervaded with horse and man scent that he could not locate the hunter, though he knew he must be near. But where? The danger of this trick was not new to the wise old buck, but he had fallen for it and now found himself in deadly peril. Hastily, he decided that safety for him lay in flight right up the hill.

Slowly he turned that way, then stopped. All at once, a hundred yards straight up the hill, the excited chattering of a chickaree squirrel burst out in the silent forest. That told the old buck that the hunter had just passed under his nest tree. The timely warning from his little friend is all that saved the buck from stopping some hot lead. Quickly he turned and bounded around the hillside out of that perilous trap to safety.

Old Long Horns had successfully eluded many a hunter before, and, even though this one was no novice, he felt that he could outsmart him, too. So he ran on to the point of timber from where he had seen the does at sunrise. From safe cover in the deep shadow of the timber, the buck watched his back track and listened intently. After awhile he heard the horse and glimpsed horse and rider coming out into the neck of the burn. Cautiously, he eased back into the forest, then made tracks as fast as he could back toward Beaver Creek. For a quarter mile he kept under cover, then deliberately went out into the open strip of the burn for a hundred yards or so, as if to cross it. Then he turned back sharply into the edge of the timber and followed it for fifty steps. There he lay down behind a log, with some dead limbs sticking up, to watch his back track.

After awhile the determined hunter, now afoot, came on slowly and cautiously. He followed the tracks out into the open area, thinking the buck had crossed it. But this time, he stopped often and looked in all directions, even straight at the buck's hiding place, but did not see him, so well was he concealed behind the log with the brushy dead limbs.

When the hunter looked the other way, the buck leaped from his bed and beat it like a flash into the dense timber, out of sight. The hunter, hearing a twig snap, turned quickly, just in time to glimpse a white rump as it disappeared in the timber, but not in time to shoot. Even as he fled, the buck's keen ears caught the sound of the hunter cursing his own carelessness.

While the buck ran at top speed for three hundred yards to make his tormentor think he was really leaving the country this time, he stopped as suddenly as he had started. Right there he turned around and, peeking through the branches of some little fir trees, began again to watch his back track. For awhile he heard the chattering of a chickaree squirrel who had been startled when the buck leaped from his bed. Then all was quiet except for the murmuring of the gentle breeze in the treetops. He waited, motionless, for a long time but no sound of the hunter came, and the wind had switched around so that he could not scent him either.

Finally, he lay down and continued to look, listen, and sniff. A snowshoe rabbit passed close by but didn't see him. Later a pair of Canadian jays perched on limbs within a few feet and made a close inspection. At last, after much bird whistle-talk, their curiosity satisfied, they flew away.

The sun was away past meridian when the patient old fellow, believing the chase had been abandoned by the hunter, got up, stretched his slender legs, and walked on slowly, still intensively alert, toward the familiar Beaver Creek area. When near the top of the range, the buck skirted the edge of a long glade and stopped at the opposite end of it, where, shielded from view by a newly wind-thrown fir, he could see quite a way back along his track.

He listened intently for the warning chatter of his little squirrel friends, but heard nothing. As the long minutes passed, it seemed more and more certain that he would be bothered no more by the pesky, red-capped hunter. Yet, though the temptation was strong, he dared not go back to find his harem, until dusk.

Well past mid-afternoon he gave up his vigil .and moved on to the east side of the range. Slowly he worked his way down the steep, timbered slope, still alert. He remembered a brush patch around the hillside a half mile or so away. There would be a good place to while away the time, feeding on leaves and tender twigs, for now he was hungry. While feeding, his thoughts turned again to the seasonal necessity for feminine companionship.

The old, long-horned buck's blood once more was warming and his nerves tingling with desire and anticipation. He also thought of those other big stout bucks whom he would have to fight and defeat decisively in order to claim his ladies. Just to prove to himself how ready for combat he really was, he started horning a fir sapling and quickly stripped it of bark and limbs. The valiant old fellow's fighting spirit was being tuned up to a high pitch as he turned from one little fir to another, horning them vigorously, demonstrating how quickly he would trim those other bucks.

Then he heard a twig crack, then the faint crunch of snow not fifty paces away. Instantly, the big buck realized that in his mock battle, he had become inexcusably careless. The persistent, red-capped hunter had waited long and patiently, then followed on. He was right there, had heard the buck, knew exactly where he was, but because of a clump of bushes, could not see him.

Instantly appraising the desperate situation, the big buck whirled around and dashed recklessly at top speed right down the hill. A few big jumps put him in the timber without being seen, and, he thought, permanently out of sight. He could not know that there was a little alley-like opening through the trees which he would have to cross and in which, seventy paces away, the hunter was standing, alert and ready.

As he crossed that narrow open space through the trees, almost in a single bound, out of the corner of his eye he glimpsed the red-capped hunter with rifle leveled. He saw a flash, heard the sharp report of the rifle, and felt a terrible shock in his loins and back. The big, long-horned buck skidded and landed with his body out of control. His back was broken and his hind quarters paralyzed. Struggling upright on his front feet, he dragged his hind quarters on down the hill to a little flat place above a dense clump of trees, and lay down, his hind legs sticking out awkwardly. He realized he was finished and that he would never get back to the Bear Creek burns to assert his right to court and caress those precious does. All the same, if his despised tormentor should come within reach, he was determined to rip him to pieces with sharp tines and front feet in spite of a broken back.

Now the sportsman was coming down the hill toward his helpless quarry, for which he had worked hard and patiently. He came slowly, cautiously, with rifle ready, not knowing how badly he had disabled the big buck. As he came in sight forty paces away, the old buck's body tensed; but he made no effort to move. They watched each other briefly. Slowly the sportsman leveled his deadly rifle for the mercy shot. As the old long-horned buck waited, there was a flash, a deafening report, and all went dark—but he felt nothing.

It was even colder and just as dark when I got back to camp that night as it had been when I left that morning. Next day, good as his promise, Dee Bibb, assisted by Homer Pickens, packed in my big old buck along with one not quite so large that Homer had killed. Arriving back at camp, Dee remarked, "Them tracks you made gitten' back to yore horse was mighty close together like you was about pooped out." He was entirely right. I was pooped out, but never had I had a better day's hunting.

11

trail riders of the wilderness

The cavalcade had made camp in mid-afternoon at Beatty's Cabin. While the sun was still warm, the women went upstream and the men down to bathe in the cold waters of the Pecos River and do the week's washing. Now, as the sun rode low over the mountains in the glowing western sky, the cooks were busy at the fire with Dutch ovens, skillets, and pots, while the packers stretched up a big tent fly and arranged the provisions beneath it. The chime and jingle of bells reverberated from across the creek, where three score saddle and pack horses had been hobbled out to graze in the tall, mountain bunch grass. The horse wranglers were busy, with ropes attached to their saddle horns, dragging in dry aspen poles for the evening bonfire.

Twenty-five riders, men and women, were scattered all over the place setting up sleeping tents, making down beds, arranging their duffle, doing this and that, or just resting from the day's ride as they awaited the evening meal.

Forest Supervisor K. D. Flock and I were sitting on a big log discussing plans for tomorrow's ride. A lone horseman, chaps flapping and spurs jingling, rode down the trail and, with an expression of utter astonishment, drew rein in front of us.

"Hallo, *Señores,* who these peoples?" he greeted and asked in one breath, in the dialect typical of some of the older Americans of Spanish and Mexican ancestry of this region.

"Hello, yourself," replied Kay. "These people are the Trail Riders of the Wilderness."

"Me no hear before now 'bout those raders weel durn nest."

Flock smiled and said, "Well, they are nice people from many places, who have come to have fun camping and riding in these mountains."

"Ees too beeg remuda, too many peeples, eat too much *pro-visiones*."

"Get down and have supper with us," I said.

"No, gracias *Senor,* me got too much hurry."

"Better stay and eat and then hurry."

"So beeg bunch peeples never see in thees mountains before. Weel durnnest raders," he exclaimed. Then, *"Adios, Senores,"* and touched spurs to his horse, which shied around the tents and set out down the canyon. There was no question but that he was most curious, as, no doubt, many others are, as to just what the Trail Riders of the Wilderness are anyway.

Indeed it was probably the biggest group of people ever to camp at Beatty's Cabin or anywhere else in the Pecos high country. That was in early September, 1949, and, for the Trail Riders of the Wilderness, the first trip into the kingdom of forests and parks of the Pecos Wilderness area. There were sixteen men and nine women Trail Riders, plus Lamar Lamb, the outfitter; Mrs. (Dr.) Key, the impeccable hostess; Forest Supervisor Kay D. Flock, Forest Ranger Bob Ground, Assistant Supervisor Ed Tucker, and me. There were three horse wranglers, two packers, and two cooks, making thirty-eight in all.

For the benefit of many who are not familiar with the wilderness areas and the Trail Riders of the Wilderness, it may be well to do a little explaining.

To get the proper perspective, we must realize that only four hundred years ago, the entire United States was a roadless wilderness inhabited only by primitive Indians. Is it any wonder, then, that a few people became alarmed some years ago lest, in a few more decades, there would be no true wilderness left where men and women could go to refresh their souls and minds in a place exactly as God made it and wholly unspoiled by the implements of modern civilization? To many of us, no church, tabernacle, or cathedral, even if gilded with all the artistry and splendor with which man is capable of adorning them, can begin to compare with the inspiring and sublime magnificence of a setting midst the scenic grandeur of an unspoiled mountain wilderness.

While there were still left a few truly primitive areas in all their majesty and pristine beauty, in 1928, the United States Forest Service designated all such major areas within the national forests, principally in the West, as wilderness areas. Thereafter, all road building and other commercial development within them was barred. God grant that they may be thus preserved in perpetuity so that posterity may continue to enjoy them and be rejuvenated and inspired by them, even as it is your and my privilege today. To commune annually with Nature, divesting our minds and souls of the grime from the grind and turmoil of modern, high-tension civilization, is a right and a privilege of which mankind should never be deprived.

For a time, these remote, untouched bits of alpine Eden were enjoyed and appreciated by but a few Nimrods and Waltonians who penetrated their fastness with gun and fly rod. Perhaps some hardy mountaineers rode their little-used trails, as did wealthy patrons of strategically located dude ranches, professional hunters, and forest rangers. But it was not until 1933 that the idea, which had been embryonic in the minds of a few wilderness enthusiasts, materialized into the organized Trail Riders of the Wilderness. From the beginning, the venerable American Forestry Association sponsored and activated the idea, which had the blessing of the U.S. Forest Service and many individuals.

From infancy, in 1933, the Trail Riders of the Wilderness has grown by leaps and bounds with a total of eleven trips scheduled for 1952. Already 113 separate expeditions have been made, in which more than 1,900 men and women have participated and more than 12,000 miles of wilderness trails explored. There are now, under lock and key against roads, occupation, and commercialization, 29 wilderness areas, embracing an area of about 11,246,000 acres. Annually, as the fine opportunity for soul-cleansing enjoyment of these remote, untamed areas becomes better known, more and more individuals and small groups, in addition to the organized Trail Riders of the Wilderness, are venturing into them, sometimes afoot but mostly on horseback with pack outfits. The recreational value and stimulating satisfaction of these trips is immeasurable, and cannot be appreciated by those less fortunate ones who have not been privileged to participate in them.

Each expedition is carefully organized on a non-profit basis, by the American Forestry Association, the riders paying an equal share in the cost of organizing and equipping the party. Only expert guides, packers, wranglers, and cooks are employed. Saddle and pack horses are safe and well-trained to mountain travel. A doctor is assigned to each expedition, and forest officers usually ride with the parties, as do representatives of the American Forestry Association. It has been my personal privilege to ride part time with four different Trail Rider expeditions, two in the Gila and two in the Pecos Wilderness area.

Naturally, it was a great personal satisfaction to me when the Pecos high country, which has meant so much to me for over a half-century, was designated as a wilderness area, thereby preserving its wild beauty and majesty inviolate against the wiles of those who would destroy it with roads, mechanized transportation, and all the artificiality that goes with them.

The party of "weel durnnest raders" now camped at Beatty's Cabin was the first expedition of the kind to try its fortune in the incomparable Pecos high country. Of the party of twenty-five, eight came from New York, three each from California, New Jersey, and Illinois, two from Ohio, one each from Indiana, Maryland, Michigan, and Florida, and two from Washington, D. C. There were representatives of many walks of life, doctors, lawyers, businessmen, secretaries, stenographers, and other occupations. Their ages ranged from twenty to sixty-five years, but here in the forest primeval it was one congenial clan with a common inheritance: the call of the wild in their hearts.

This group had assembled in the ancient city of Santa Fe as the jumping off place for the wilderness ride. My good friend, Erie Kauffman, then editor of *American Forests,* was the American Forestry Association representative in charge of the trip. In the evening, the party held a little meeting at La Fonda Hotel to get acquainted and get organized for the trip, scheduled to start at eight-thirty o'clock next morning. Since this was the first trip for many of them, although there were some veterans, Mr. Kauffman gave a little talk relative to their equipment and organization on the trail and in camp, and a few pointers on how to get the most out of the trip.

The medical officer, Dr. J. Berkeley Gordan, medical director of the New Jersey State Hospital, gave a talk in which he reassured everyone that they would be well taken care of. He anticipated the worst trouble to be expected would be sunburn and some saddle-chafed legs, stiff knees, etc., and made some timely suggestions for their avoidance and remedy.

Forest Supervisor Flock briefly outlined the itinerary for the trip and spoke of the part the U. S. Forest Service plays in guarding the wilderness areas and assisting in the Trail Rider expeditions. He told the group that most of the camps would be at elevations of 9,300 feet or more, and, hence, the nights would be quite chilly, and advised everyone to wear long under-wear with warm outer clothing and to have good raincoats.

I was called upon to tell them something about the wildlife and fishing resources of the area and the fishing equipment they might need. I said it was not likely that so large a party would see much game, despite the fact that there are plenty of elk, mule deer, and black bear in the area, as well as some bobcats, coyotes, foxes, martens and, possibly, a mountain lion or two. Wild turkeys, blue grouse, whistling marmots and pikas in the rock slides, snowshoe rabbits, chickaree squirrels and other rodents, and birds of many species also might be seen.

After that there was a question and answer session through which we became better acquainted with each other. Ten o'clock was upon us before we knew it and the party broke up to get ready for the call to boots and saddles on the morrow.

While Cowles, on the Pecos River, at the end of the road is the principal gateway to the Wilderness area, we had arranged for this expedition to enter from the west side. Lamar Lamb, manager of Mountain View Ranch, at Cowles, had the saddle and pack horses brought over the Santa Fe Range to the end of the road, at the ski run in Aspen Basin, fifteen miles east of Santa Fe. Promptly at eight o'clock, duffle bags and bedrolls were loaded in a truck and the riders followed in cars, enjoying the scenic trip up through Hyde Park to Aspen Basin, where the horses were waiting.

Big stout horses were assigned to the heavier riders, smaller ones for the others, and extra gentle ones for those unaccustomed to riding. I am confident that no actual posterior measurements were taken, yet the needs of each rider, for size and type of saddle, were tactfully appraised and allocations made accordingly. Some of the riders set right to work in adjusting the stirrups as to length, while others had to have it done for them. Each saddle and horse was numbered so there would be no mixup of horses, saddles, and riders on succeeding days.

The cars returned to Santa Fe and by ten o'clock we were happily on the trail, beginning an exciting and inspiring thirteen-day trek through a marvelously fine mountain wilderness. The long, winding trail led up the mountain through a forest of slender, white-barked aspen interspersed with clumps of spruce and an occasional flower-dotted park. Across the canyon, to the south, bleached logs, scattered over a large area, glistening in the sun bore mute evidence of the ravages of a destructive forest fire which occurred three-quarters of a century or more before.

Crossing the first high ridge, the caravan continued its journey through spruce-covered slopes to a grassy opening beside a rivulet that went tumbling down the mountain, where we stopped for lunch. The plan was to make the first day a short, easy trip to get all riders accustomed to their mounts and saddles without getting too tired. As we lounged on the sun-bathed slope Canadian jays whistle-talked in the trees nearby and, occasionally, ventured within a few feet of us, picking up scraps of bread that were tossed their way. Striped chipmunks scurried along the logs here and there, while big fat ground squirrels sat straight up on their haunches, using their front feet, as expertly as we would our hands, to hold food to their mouths and to crowd it into the pockets of their already bulging jaws. In the slide rocks above us, a marmot poked his grey head up over a boulder, intermittently piercing the air with his sharp whistle to warn his clan that intruders were about to invade their domain.

Someone discovered red raspberries growing here and there next to the rocks and logs. The ripe wild fruit was so delicious that when the call came to remount and get under way again, there was general reluctance to leave the spot.

The first camp site was on the head of Nambe Creek, a mile and a half west of Puerto Nambe", a gap between Penitente Peak and towering Santa Fe Baldy, through which we would pass tomorrow to get over onto the Pecos drainage. Since it was early afternoon and we were ahead of the pack outfit, I suggested that we ride up on the shoulder of Santa Fe Baldy above the last timber, where we could look out over the vast expanse of mountains and canyons, parks and forests that were to be our home for the next twelve days.

During the steep, tedious climb we had to stop often to let the horses regain their breath, but, at last, approached the crest of the ridge, which breaks off abruptly on the east side, affording an unobstructed view of much of the fine Pecos high country. Riding near me were Laura Stephens and Dr. Elfenbaum, and, just*before we reached the top, I suggested that they close their eyes tightly and keep them closed. When we were squarely on top and the whole magnificent panorama was before us, I said, "Now, look." The breath-taking gorgeous splendor of the mosaic of forests, parks, aspens, old burns, and peaks so suddenly presented left them gasping for words to express their amazement and gratification. The towering, rugged Truchas Peaks were hidden by an intervening ridge, but away across the horseshoe basin which comprises the Pecos high country, with its labyrinth of ridges and canyons, could be seen the Rio de la Casa divide and, far to the south of it, Spring Mountain, both of which were on our itinerary.

Erie Kauffman, daddy of the Trail Rider trips, had perhaps been a bit skeptical as to our having a worthwhile wilderness area here in the Pecos high country. So, after we had all looked for a long time, enjoying the marvelous view, and Kay Flock and I had pointed out spots of interest and the general route we would follow, I asked, "Erie, what do you think now, do we have a wilderness area?" "Yes," he stated, without hesitation, "you have, and I would say a very splendid one."

Back at the camp the cooks were busy getting supper. Beds were made down in the open or under trees, the women on one side of the creek and the men a couple of hundred yards away on the other. After a fine supper, a big bonfire was built and everyone gathered around it to talk, tell stories, and enjoy the billowing fire. Far across the Rio Grande Valley to the west, we could see the twinkling lights of Los Alamos, the new city in the Jemez Mountains, famed as the cradle and home of the atomic bomb.

Some of the saddles had been left nearby, and one young lady was seen examining the one she had ridden that day.

"Is there something wrong with your saddle?" someone asked.

"I guess not," she replied, "I was just wondering why the soft sheepskin lining was put on the side that goes next to the horse."

When the laughter had subsided, I told them the story about a young lady from the East who had been on a rather long ride. When she got back to town, she went into a drugstore, whereupon an exceedingly bowlegged ex-cowboy clerk pranced up and asked, "May I help you?" She said, "I would like a can of talcum powder, please." The very bowlegged clerk turned and, as he started toward the back of the store, said, "Walk this way, lady, please." "Wait a minute," she exclaimed, "if I could walk that way, I wouldn't need the talcum powder."

Our destination the next day was a camp site selected in the deep alpine forest, near Stewart Lake. The trail led through Puerto Nambe onto the steep, timbered slopes above the head of many-pronged Holy Ghost Canyon, a fine tributary of the Pecos River. Conversation lagged, for, through the trees, everyone was enjoying to the utmost glimpses of the entrancing panorama which lay below and across from us. Down, down, down for a couple of miles, then, all of a sudden, we came to Spirit Lake, nestling placidly in a little pocket in the alpine forest. There we stopped for a brief rest, but Lamar and one or two others lingered to fish for cutthroat trout.

The rest of us went on to a fork in the trail, two or three miles above camp, where we turned back up the hill, following the many switchbacks of the steep scenic trail toward Lake Katherine, gem of all our timberline lakes. When we were nearly there, at a spot where the trail crosses a little pond, we saw in the mud fresh tracks of a bear, some deer, elk, and a coyote. As we made the last steep climb to the lake, marmots scurried to their dens, their shrill whistles warning all of our approach. Near the lake, we saw some little rock conies, or pika, with the characteristic little pile of grass laid out to dry near their winter dens.

I have no words to describe the thrilling wild beauty of Lake Katherine. It is splendid and spectacular. The elevation is about 11,500 feet, the area about twenty acres, and its waters, blue as the sky above it, are sixty-five feet deep. It snuggles up close to the precipitous, boulder strewn base of majestic Santa Fe Baldy, while the opposite shore is lined with spruce trees, tall and straight as flagpoles. The view out over the mountain country to the east is unexcelled.

Seated on rocks and boulders, we ate. our noonday lunch beside the rippling waters. A pair of golden eagles soared about overhead while a chickaree squirrel chattered and scolded in his nest tree nearby. An occasional swirl on the surface of the lake inspired some of us to try our luck fishing for the gamey cutthroat trout with which the State Game Department stocks the lake. But they were not striking well and only two or three of the twelve- to fifteen-inch beauties were taken. Meanwhile, Lamar Lamb, we later learned, had caught the limit of fifteen fish at Spirit Lake.

The zigzag trail down the mountain seemed even steeper than it did coming up, and some walked and led their horses over the worst of it. The camp in the forest was comfortable enough, and we had a fine supper of beefsteak, beans, and Dutch-oven biscuits, which everyone enjoyed immensely. The bonfire that evening, with its blue smoke spiraling up through the stately trees, was, perhaps, the best we had anywhere on the trip. Besides the usual stories, songs, and jokes, Erie Kauffman told us the story of the wilderness areas and how the Trail Riders of the Wilderness idea was born and grew up.

Despite all this, for some reason, the camp site in the forest did not appeal to the group and it was decided that future camps should be in open, grassy parks or meadows with a good supply of water nearby.

The third day's ride was a long one through fine country, with Pecos Baldy Lake as our destination. A couple of hours' ride through timber and glades brought us to Horse Thief Meadows, a charming, untamed beauty spot. Here we paused to rest a while, admire the many varieties of wild flowers growing in profusion, and to take pictures of individuals, the party, and the country. Right then and there, the riders, whose opinions are regularly asked, recommended Horse Thief Meadows instead of Stewart Lake forest as next year's camp site.

Another two-hour ride, across the upper Panchuela Creek and Rito Perro, brought us to a nice cold spring in a beautiful aspen park near Jack's Creek, where we stopped for lunch. A fire was built and both coffee and tea were brewed, which greatly improved the sandwich lunch. As we lingered here, low, threatening clouds drifted in over the peaks and we fretted a little because the pack string had not overtaken us. We feared something might have gone wrong and it looked as if we might need the tents.

We rode on anyway up Jack's Creek, through forest and glade, toward Baldy Lake. A light airplane circled low overhead and we surmised its pilot might be looking for us. In one opening we suddenly came upon two hen turkeys with about thirty half-grown poults feeding on grasshoppers in the tall bunch grass. Everyone got a glimpse of them and were thrilled with the experience. This, the Merriam or mountain turkey, is native only to the mountains of the southwestern states and northern Mexico. When we started on, Mr. Snadjar's horse got into a big yellow jackets' nest, and of all the pawing, kicking, stomping, and snorting you ever saw, that old bay horse did it, but Snadjar sat tight until he could get him out of the buzzing and stinging mess.

By the time we got to Baldy Lake, a cold, drizzling rain had set in and there were no tents, for the pack outfit had not yet arrived. Lamar, who had gone on ahead, had a big fire going under some trees and we stood around it waiting for the pack string. We found the plane we had seen had dropped a bundle of recent newspapers which we read in the rain. Mrs. Key, our pretty, always handsomely dressed hostess was most solicitous for everyone's welfare but in the absence of tents, cooks, and provisions, there wasn't much anyone could do. The damp, chill fog banked in thickly and it began to get dark, but still no camp outfit. What was wrong? They couldn't have missed the trail; or had they? Some began to get really worried, so Lamar and I started back to look for the outfit, but just then they arrived and the party perked up at once.

When hot coffee and a quickly prepared supper, mostly of canned goods, were served the world looked a lot brighter. Soon tents were set up and beds made down inside by flashlight. Despite the fog and occasional drizzle of rain, we had a nice evening around the bonfire. This time everyone in turn was asked to tell just who he was, where he was from, what his education and training were, his occupation, and hobby. We were now really getting acquainted.

The fourth day, camp was not moved. Some wanted to rest, some fished in Baldy Lake, nine of the group made the strenuous trip to top of South Truchas Peak, elevation 13,110. The last two of the six miles had to be made afoot. I took some of the party over to the escarpment overlooking Cebadilloso Canyon to contemplate the marvelous view of the beautiful canyon itself, and the Beatty's Cabin region, with its peaks and parks, canyons and ridges, alpine forests and aspen slopes. After a while I tossed a rock off down the steep slope toward a clump of trees and up jumped a fine pair of mule deer bucks, their massive antlers in the velvet. They bounded off down the hill like rubber balls.

The fifth day we had an uneventful ride down Jack's Creek to Round Mountain, where we had a jolly half-mile gallop and then posed for pictures. Then we took the trail to Beatty's Cabin, which goes through some of the biggest, tallest, and finest gray-barked, trembling-leafed aspen forests to be found in all the mountains. We made camp in front of the Game Department and Forest Service administrative cabins, across the creek from the site of the original Beatty's Cabin. It was here that the lone native horseman, curious about the "weel durnnest raders," came along.

Of all the camp sites, this Trail Riders group and the two succeeding ones, liked Beatty's Cabin the best. Here, at the junction of the main Pecos and Rito del Padre, there is ample opportunity for fishing in three directions from camp, an abundance of water, though pretty cold, for bathing and washing clothes, and ample room in the flower-studded meadows and parks, all in a remote peaceful setting.

A packer had come up from the Mountain View Ranch with fresh supplies and we had fried chicken, gravy, and Dutch-oven biscuits and nobody complained about it. At the fire that evening it was Kay Flock's turn to do the entertaining and he did a bang-up job. He told of the origin and purpose of the national forests, their administration by the Forest Service, their protection from fire, how livestock grazing is regulated, how timber is sold and selectively harvested, how very valuable the mountain watersheds are, and how this one here provides water for irrigation three hundred miles downstream.

The seventh day, camp was moved five or six miles up the main stream, while the riders were to make a circuitous trip and get in late that evening. I was asked to lead the party over a partly trailless route. I guided them up Cebadilloso Canyon to the amphitheater at its head, then over the steep ridge to the north, and around under the precipitous ridge, with the uniform, horizontal outcroppings of limestone, which the natives call *Bordo Lajado*. Then we meandered through parks and thickets down the South Azul to the Chimayosos Creek, where we had lunch. Several bunches of blue grouse were flushed out of the tall grass with a suddenness and whirring of wings that startled both horses and riders.

It had been a strenuous half-day's ride and the bodies and legs of some were crying for relief, not W.P.A. either. But with an hour-and-a-half rest, everyone was ready for boots and saddles again.

It was with the utmost regret and disappointment that I had to leave the party at this time. I had to return to Santa Fe and go at once to attend the annual conference of the International Association of Game, Fish and Conservation Commissioners in Winnipeg, Canada. It had been altogether a most enjoyable trip and I would have liked to continue on to the end. The Riders constituted one of the finest groups of people it had ever been my privilege to ride and camp with.

Where did the cavalcade of riders of wilderness trails go from there? Where did they make their last camp? At which end of the trail were they met with cars? Well, I wasn't there so any answer would be hearsay. Better you come and make the trip and find out for yourself. I'll guarantee it will be worth while.

12

outlaw
cabin

The 1933 deer and elk season had closed on November 10. All the cattle and horses which summer graze in the area were supposed to have been rounded up in October and driven out to winter range or feed lots. The Pecos high country was about ready to be tucked in under soft, white blankets to sleep through the long, silent winter. Like a fond mother who takes a last good night peek at her sleeping children before leaving them for the night, Forest Ranger J. W. Johnson decided to make one last round of the Pecos high country. Perhaps it was just because he loved the country or maybe he had a hunch that all was not well.

All the same, on November 11 Ranger Johnson left Pan-chuela Ranger Station mounted on his sturdy, sure-footed horse, Smokey, and, leading a pack horse, rode to Beatty's Cabin, where he spent the night alone. There was some snow on the ground and it was bitter cold but in the cabin he was warm and comfortable. Early the next morning, the Ranger set out up the Pecos to cover the country above the falls, intending to come back by way of the head of Jaroso Creek and Rito Padre.

The frost crystals on the crusted snow glistened in the early morning light as he left the cabin, and the mush ice which clogged the river at the ford in front of the cabin made the crossing very difficult. The snow crunched and squeaked under Smokey's hoofs as he plodded up the trail to the head of the river. In one of the many parks in the aspens a fine bunch of mule deer bounded away as horse and rider approached. The tracks and beds of a few elk were noted in the snow along the way. At one place, a big mountain coyote crossed the trail and ran up through the bunch grass on the hillside, but by the time Johnson got his trusted lueger out of the holster beneath his tightly buttoned, wool-lined coat, the coyote was out of range.

Passing through the drift fence at the bend in the river away above the falls, Ranger Johnson took the trail up toward the Rio de la Casa divide. He noticed some horse tracks crossing the trail and wondered who had been so careless as to leave their horses here, because they were very liable to be marooned in the first really deep snow, as Don Juan Climaco's horses had been many years before. There are lots of grassy bench lands interspersed through the timber in the Rincón at the head of the river, and he swung to the left to ride through some of the larger ones. After a little while he headed Smokey up a steep hill to go from one bench up to the next one above. There he again saw that horses had been pawing away the snow to graze on the grass buried beneath it. Riding across this little snow-covered bench-land park, he suddenly came around a dense clump of bushy spruce trees near its edge and, to his utter amazement, found himself in the very yard of a well-concealed, half-dug-out log cabin. Not only that, but there, only a few feet away, was a young man unsaddling a horse, while just inside the door of the cabin stood a second young man with a .30-30 rifle at the ready.

Instantly Johnson sized up the situation as a vicious game poacher's camp, for strewn about the place were the heads of a buck, doe, and fawn, and a big bull elk. He had not even suspected that a cabin had been built anywhere in the area, nor that such flagrant violations of the game law could be going on. Neither did the Department of Game and Fish nor anyone else, for that matter. The fellows were natives of Spanish-American blood but spoke some English. While Ranger Johnson had been startled, it was evident that they, too, had been taken by surprise and were scared badly.

Johnson tried to find out who they were, why they were there, where they lived, but with no success. He tried to talk them into putting the rifle away, speaking to them both in English and Spanish, but they stood their ground menacingly. He soon saw that it was hopeless to get them to give up, and since they were scared, it was obvious to him that they were really dangerous. It would have been foolhardy for the Ranger, good officer and woodsman as he was, to try to get his pistol from the holster beneath his heavy, tightly-buttoned coat to force the issue, because they had him well covered with the rifle. Soundly acting on the theory that discretion is the better part of valor, Ranger Johnson did just exactly what I would have done, he turned and rode away.

Once out of sight, he made Smokey quicken his pace and rode at a pretty good clip to Beatty's Cabin. There he fed Smokey, got a bite to eat himself, and then hurried on back to Panchuela Station, twelve miles distant, where he arrived quite late that evening. It so happened that I was State Game Warden at the time, and Johnson at once phoned me what had occurred. The next morning I called in two of my top field wardens, Tom Holder and Bert Baca, and sent them up there with Ranger Johnson to bring in the outlaws if they were still there, or follow them out and get them if they had left.

I cautioned them to use the greatest tact and judgment, for I didn't want any shooting scrape if it could be avoided. They were warned particularly about a possible ambush; and were told definitely to report back from somewhere not later than the next evening. They were to go to Beatty's Cabin the first night, and be at the outlaw cabin as early as possible the next morning.

That day passed, and the next, and no word came from the officers. On the morning of the third day, I began to worry lest they had been ambushed or had otherwise met with foul play. It didn't seem reasonable to suppose that all three could have been put out of commission by two young hoodlums, but why had they not reported back? If the men had been followed out to the other side of the range, there would be a telephone at Mora or some nearby town. On the other hand, if they had found the outlaws at the cabin, either on the first or second day, there had been plenty of time to get them and get back. By evening I was getting pretty much worked up and condemned myself for not having gone along, yet I knew very well that they could do as good a job, or better, in a pinch than I could.

By ten o'clock that night I decided to do something about it. I called Skipper Viles at the Mountain View Ranch, near Pan-chuela Ranger Station and forty-six miles from Santa Fe, and asked him to get three good saddle horses ready. Then I called Homer Pickens, another one of my field men, now Assistant State Game Warden, and asked him to go with me. I also called Dee Bibb, a big, good-natured cowboy at Tererro, a few miles below the Mountain View Ranch, explained what the setup was, and asked him to go along.

"What time you be out?" he asked.

"About midnight or a little after," I said.

"It'll be cold enough to freeze the ears off of a brass monkey but I'll be rarin' to go." Then, as an afterthought, he said, "Reckon there ain't no use takin' my peejamas along 'cause we won't git there in time to go to bed." I agreed there would be no use in it.

At a little after 2:00 A.M., the three of us, on that dark, zero cold night, left Mountain View Ranch for Beatty's Cabin. We were dressed for the cold night, but, even so, as we crossed Hamilton Mesa the sharp wintry breeze stung our faces and numbed our fingers and toes. The crusted snow, from six inches to a foot deep, made travel slow and our anxiety for the safety of our buddies, coupled with the ungodly hour of the night, made a really dismal, dreary trip of it. Dee had a dozen theories as to what had happened, such as, "I'll betcha dollars to doughnuts them old boys got a taste of that wild elk meat and turned outlaw their own selves, and, damn it, we'll have to bring in five hombres instead of two"; or, "They just had to kill them fellers and the ground is froze so durn hard buryin' them is quite a chore."

Only the faintest sign of dawn was showing in the east when we came in sight of the cabin, but our spirits rose and our anxiety faded for a light was shining in the window. Three saddled horses were at the hitching pole, and when we got there, Dee let out a tonsil straining war whoop that could be heard for miles. Instantly, the cabin door was flung open and Johnson greeted us with, "Who the hell is there?"

"Just a 'posey' searchin' for three babes in the woods," chided Dee.

There they were, safe and sound, breakfast over, drinking a last cup of coffee before starting back to the outlaw cabin again. They related this story: When they arrived at the outlaw cabin, three days before, they found the outlaws had left, taking only a part of the contraband meat and a part of their camp outfit, hence they thought the fellows would be back after the rest of it. They had been going up to the cabin each morning and waiting all day for them to arrive. The officers had started to follow the outlaws out but soon found that some cattle and horses-remnants of the October round up—had been driven out over their trail and they surmised it would be very difficult at the villages at the base of the mountain to tell where the men had gone. They had found nothing about the camp to indicate who they were or from whence they came. "So," Bert said, "we decided to wait till they came back; we never once thought of your worrying about us."

"Oh, no? Well, we didn't; it was your families we were worrying about," I replied sarcastically.

After a hurried breakfast we all set out for the outlaw cabin, hoping that the culprits had returned. It was another three-hour ride up there and still a mighty frosty morning. We approached the cabin with caution but soon found that no one had been back. We all looked the place over very carefully but the only thing we found to help identify the fugitives was a scrap of wrapping paper with the word, "Mora," on it. We concluded their post office was Mora, a little town on the east side of the mountain twenty-eight miles north of Las Vegas.

In looking the place over, we found evidence that, in addition to killing deer and elk, they had been trapping for fur-bearing animals. There were bobcat and coyote carcasses scattered about, and, of much more interest, we discovered the carcasses of two pine martens. Now pine martens are exceedingly rare in New Mexico, occurring only in a few of the high mountain areas such as this at elevations above 10,500 feet, but their fur is quite valuable. It was not likely that a half dozen martens had been taken in the state that year. Those facts gave us an idea.

"If we can find where they sold those marten skins, we can find our men," I said.

"Yes, but they could have shipped them out of state to any one of a dozen fur houses," Pickens surmised.

"Not likely, though, since there is a pretty good fur buyer in Las Vegas; I'll bet they sold them there."

"Yeah, that's right, but he probably won't give his customers away."

"If he bought them, he'll tell us without knowing he is giving anybody away because martens are not protected," I said.

We saw no hope of the outlaws coming back so we rode to Beatty's Cabin for a three-o'clock dinner, then on out to the Mountain View Ranch, and thence to Santa Fe by car, arriving at 10:00 P.M and I know one guy who was pretty well tired out. When Dee left us at Tererro, he said, "I'll betcha my 'peejamas' will be waitin' at the door to welcome me."

A few days later we drove over to Las Vegas and went straight to my friend, the fur buyer. "Joe, we want you to settle a bet," I said as we shook hands. "Ranger Johnson here says there are some pine martens in New Mexico and I bet him ten bucks there aren't."

"Well, you lose. I'm afraid you made a bad bet," Joe stated.

"I'll still say there are no marten in the state. I'm Game Warden and I ought to know."

"I can prove you are wrong."

"How can you prove it, you never saw one."

"No, not the animal, but I sometimes buy the skins. I bought two last week. Come back here, I'll show you," and we all went with him to the little warehouse at the back of the store, where he showed us two beautiful skins.

"Where the hell did they come from?" I demanded.

"Some place on the high mountain above Mora."

"Well, I'll be damned; who caught them?"

"Two native fellows. Come on up to the office and I'll give you their names." Soon we had the information we needed.

"O. K., Johnson, you win," and I handed over a ten dollar bill and we walked out of the store without Joe suspecting in the least that the bet was all a farce. When we got to the car Johnson gave the ten bucks back.

At Mora, we swore out warrants for the arrest of the culprits and had no trouble in finding one of them right away. He was not at all belligerent now. We went to the other's house, but his mother said he wasn't home. We thought he was and said we would wait. With typical Spanish-American hospitality, the old lady asked us in and to sit down. Speaking in Spanish, I inquired where Jose was. She didn't know. I asked when he would be back. She didn't know that either. From her attitude, though, we thought the man was right there in the house. Johnson and Pickens went out and looked around the sheds and barns.

"*Vale mas que no nos engana*," "Better not deceive us," I said, "for we are going to wait right here until he comes if it's an hour or a week."

"*Bueno, haga como quieres.*" "All right, do as you please."

We talked about her farm, her little bunch of stock, the weather, and I complimented her on her nicely kept house. At long last, the affable old lady excused herself and went out into the kitchen. In half an hour she came back and said she thought her son might be back soon. We said we hoped so. Pretty soon

José sheepishly poked his head around the door from another room where he had been hiding all the time and surrendered to us.

The two were tried, convicted, and fined $300 each and given a six months' jail sentence, which they served at hard labor.

An interesting sequel is that the fellows left the state for a year or so, then returned and built another well-concealed cabin in Rincon Bonito, across the ridge from the original cabin on the Rio de la Casa side. Department of Game and Fish patrolman in the area at that time was L. W. (Speed) Simmons, a top woodsman and officer, who discovered the cabin one summer. Late that fall when snows lay deep over the high country he rode in halfway to Beatty's Cabin, and when the horse couldn't go any farther he turned him loose to go home alone, while he continued, on web snowshoes.

Setting out early next morning he made the long, grueling climb out of the canyon, went around the ridge east of the Pecos, and over the divide to the cabin in Rincón Bonito, a distance of nine miles. He arrived in mid-afternoon and found the cabin was being occupied, but no one was home at the moment. He looked the place over and found it as clean as a hound's tooth, with no sign of game law violations. At dark, the same two young men came back to camp, proudly displaying a pine marten they had legally trapped, not realizing it was a pair of these little animals that had trapped them a few years before.

Although invited to stay all night, Speed chose to return to Beatty's Cabin by moonlight, since the snow would be well frozen and not stick to the webs, there to spend what little was left of the night in the warmth of his own bed. Only a man of great vigor, determination, and devotion to duty could, or would, have made such a long grueling trip. Evidently the young outlaws had learned their lesson and were sticking to legal trapping.

13

what's in a name?

Perhaps no locality has as many unusual and distinctive names for its creeks and peaks as the Pecos high country. Of course, it also has the usual run of names but here we find them with interesting and unique variations. While almost every mountain range has its Baldy Peak, here we have four of them: Santa Fe Baldy, Santa Barbara Baldy, Glorieta Baldy, and Pecos Baldy. By translation, the religious background of three of them is revealed, for it would be Holy Faith Baldy, Saint Barbara Baldy, and Little Heaven or Heavenly Baldy. Trout creeks are common, but here we have Truchas (Trout) Peaks instead, undoubtedly so named because the many creeks radiating from the base of the peaks like the spokes of a wheel from the hub are all fine, native cutthroat trout waters.

Everywhere there are Willow creeks but here we find them in both English and Spanish: Willow Creek, entering the Pecos River at Tererro; and Rito Jaroso, literally Willowy Creek, joining the Pecos below the falls, three miles above Beatty's Cabin. Likewise, just plain Bear Creek is found here, as elsewhere, but there is also the interesting variation Rito Del Oso (Creek of the Bear), where Naturalist L. L. Dyche had his "Bear Trail" camp. From a biological standpoint, it is inevitable that we would have a Calf Creek, for there is a Cow Creek and a Bull Creek with no formidable barrier between.

If there were no other evidence that the wapiti, that lordly game animal commonly called elk, was indigenous to the area, the fact that we have both a prominent mountain and a fine trout stream named Elk, would be indicative of that fact. Noisy Brook is a more or less common name, and, indeed, a most fascinating one, so, naturally, the Pecos high country has its Noisy Brook, too, which comes tumbling noisily off the steep side of Round Mountain. Not satisfied with that, some one christened another brook with the equally interesting and euphonious counterpart, Rito Ruidoso (Noisy Creek) .

Las Vegas, (the meadows), is the name of a city in both Nevada and New Mexico, while here one of the prettiest, flower-spangled spots in the whole area is called Vega Bonita (Pretty Meadow). Valle (pronounced "vie yay") Medio, meaning valley in between or middle valley, instead of being a valley between two mountains is the name used to designate the high, grassy-topped mountain between Bear Creek and the Rito de las Trampas. Rito de las Trampas (Creek of the Traps), is so named because in the early days it was a favorite place to trap bear.

Rito de los Esteros (Creek of the Marshes) is rightly named because of the boggy marshes at its source west of Spring Mountain, many of which used to be difficult to cross on horseback before trails were cut through the windfalls around them. Speaking of Spring Mountain, the name is appropriate because of the permanent ice cold spring at the north end of a half-mile-long segment of the range, which is only slightly higher than the spring itself. It is nearer to the top of a mountain than any spring I know.

Where else but in the Pecos high country could one find such unusual and intriguing names of topographic features as Rito de los Chimayosos, Rito Cebadilloso, Rito del Padre, Cerrito del Padre, Holy Ghost Creek, Spirit Lake, Lake Katherine, Chaparrito Creek, Rito Azul, Rito Perro, Rio de la Casa, Rincón Bonito, Palocientos, Panchuela Creek, Horse Thief Meadows, Truchas Peaks, Lost Bear Lake, and many others? And there are some interesting stories and a bit of history back of some of them, too.

Take Lost Bear Lake, for instance. In June, 1908, I was camped on Spring Mountain to hunt bear, for I was out of a job and there was a twenty-dollar bounty on bear. Besides, the fur there in the high mountains was still prime and worth considerable. I sold one grizzly hide for fifty dollars. Anyway, one dark, drizzling, foggy day, with a couple of dogs, I followed a big grizzly bear trail from the head of the Rito de las Trampas, west of my camp, northward across ridges and canyons toward the very head of the Pecos. Up near the source of the river darkness overtook us and the dogs, my horse, and I had to give it up and lay out all night, without blankets or provisions, returning to camp the next day. While on the trail of the bear, I was too interested and busy to pay much attention to where we were as he led us through some of the ruggedest, loggiest, and most densely timbered country he could find. Besides, it was a dark and foggy day and one could tell the directions only by the moss on the trees. Somewhere along the trail the old bear passed by a little lake in the dense spruce and fir timber on a north or northwest hillside. He stepped in the mud at the edge of the lake and made tracks six inches deep with his long feet. Several times afterward I tried to find the little lake but could never go back to it.

In 1934, when camped at Beatty's Cabin with Forest Ranger J. W. Johnson, I told him the story of the bear and the lake and described the general area in which it had to be. Johnson said, "Elliott, if you are not just telling me a big windy, I can find that lake."

I assured him that as far as that story was concerned, I might be a direct descendant of George Washington.

The next summer, Johnson took a pair of binoculars and rode to the top of the Santa Barbara divide, where he could look southward into all the north exposures in the region I had described to him. Sure enough, he finally detected a depression in a steep, heavily timbered hillside a couple of miles above Pecos Falls. When he rode to it, he found the little lake of the forest just as I had described it to him. He said he thought he could still see the twenty-six-year-old grizzly bear tracks in the mud. He named it Lost Bear Lake, appropriate because I lost both the bear and the lake.

The Rito de los Chimayosos, that is to say, the creek of the people of Chimayó, is one of the main sources of the Pecos River, rising in a series of springs and marshes at the east base of Truchas Peaks. The story is that it got its name because the people of Chimayó, a little village eighteen miles west of Truchas Peaks, like their red-skinned predecessors, used to come over there to hunt. Later the villagers brought sheep to graze there in the marshes and timber-line parks. The people of Chimayó of Mexican or Spanish ancestry, that is, the Chimayosos, have become quite famous for the very fine, vividly-colored, and artistically-designed Chimayó blankets which they weave.

The Rito Azul, a two-pronged tributary of the Chimayosos, could not have been given a better-suited name. The Engel-mann spruce and alpine fir forests, surrounding the meadows and bunch-grass parks, are the bluest of any in the whole area. The double canyon might, however, have been named Rito Azul for the gentians, blue as the sky, which bloom in profusion in some of the meadows.

Rito Cebadilloso with equal propriety might have been christened with a more savory name, for the tall blue larkspur grows and blooms as profusely as the broad-leafed, white-blossomed skunk cabbage to which the name alludes. In the event the creek were to be renamed in Spanish, the most appropriate alternative would be Rito Espuela de Caballero (Larkspur Creek).

There would have to be a Beatty's Creek, Beatty's Parks, and east Beatty's Parks, and one may readily guess how they got their names. One Baldy was left out; it is Baldy Lake, a fine trout lake snuggling up close to the base of double-crested Pecos Baldy. Originally, this was just a little shallow pond of an acre or two in extent and slimy with water dogs. The pond was in the bottom of a much larger natural basin with a hole in one side where the water ran out. It was a big crevice in the shattered limestone formation and one could climb down in it for thirty feet or more. The Department of Game and Fish plugged the hole and then developed a ten or twelve-acre lake well-suited to trout. Yellowstone cutthroat trout were packed in to it in cans on pack mules and it has become one of the finest little fishing spots in all the remote wilderness area.

Another such underground waterway is to be found on Cave Creek where the entire flow of the little creek runs into a descending cave at the side of the canyon and comes out again a half-mile below. This, of course, gives rise to the name, and it is literally a creek in a cave. Farther down country there is the Spanish counterpart, Rito de la Cueva.

Horse Thief Meadows, which is a mighty nice place to camp where one may always be sure of a mess of eight-inch brook or native trout for supper, many years ago was found, by a band of outlaws, to have advantages for other, less worthy, uses. The designated area consists of a secluded strip of meadows and bunch grass parks, three miles long, on the middle fork of Panchuela Creek, entirely surrounded by the densest kind of spruce and fir forests with an under story of tangled logs. The hidden haven was not easy of access before the Forest Service built a trail into it from Cave Creek, on the south, and out of it to the west and northeast. Even today, the canyon below for a considerable distance is barely passable afoot. The upper end of the long opening is characterized by grassy marshes dotted with a great variety of wild flowers and patches of short mountain willows growing along the beaver dammed stream. Below, the lush bunch grass, with drooping, oat-like heads, on the northeast side of the creek constitutes as succulent a pasture as could be desired, with the advantage of being enclosed with natural barriers.

As the story goes, an organized band of horse thieves, most likely a part of the infamous Vicente Silva gang of Las Vegas in the 1880's, found the spot and used it as a natural holding pasture for stolen horses. It seems that valuable horses would be stolen from the big ranchers or other owners in the Las Vegas area and brought to this secluded spot, where they would be rebranded or the brands changed, whichever best suited the purpose. Naturally, in the cool, succulent pasture the horses would very soon become located and be content to stay right there without being herded. The robbers found it to their advantage to leave them there unattended until the new brands had all healed and haired over. Then they would come back and take their ill-gotten loot over the mountains to the west and dispose of it in the Espanola and Chama valleys, the new brands making it possible to give acceptable bills of sale.

It is reported that this went on for several years, but, finally, after a valuable stallion had been stolen, along with a number of other good horses, the owner and the sheriff from Las Vegas trailed the bandits with the stolen horses to the hidden meadows. There they found and recovered their newly branded animals, but the thieves had already departed for parts unknown and never were captured. From that (actual or legendary) day on, the place has been known as Horse Thief Meadows.

It is intriguing to speculate upon how Holy Ghost Creek came by its unusual name but, whatever the real explanation is, it has not come to my knowledge. I was told once that the big cave at the mouth of the creek was responsible. This big hole, which extends three-quarters of a mile into the side of the mountain, was supposed to be full of ghosts, hence, the name of Holy Ghost. If that were the case, it would seem Ghosty Hole would be more appropriate.

For a more plausible explanation, let's trace the stream to its source. There we find impressive little Spirit Lake nestling down in the dense forest with the tall moss-covered trees growing right up to the water's edge. The beautiful song of the Audubon hermit thrush, at sunset, alone breaks the oppressive silence of the forest. The treetops and leisurely-drifting clouds dimly reflected in the shadowy waters lend an eerie enchantment to the scene, which might well cause a religious person to contemplate upon the Creator—the Holy Spirit—and so christen the lake.

I used to hear the old native Spanish Americans refer to the lake as La Laguna del Espiritu Santo (The Lake of the Holy Spirit), or Holy Ghost. It was, perhaps, originally so christened and the creek naturally took the same name, while the lake's name was shortened to just Spirit Lake. The theory is strengthened by the fact that this area is in the Sangre de Cristo Range, so named by pioneer ecclesiastics who, viewing the lofty mountain tops bathed in crimson glow at sunrise, were reminded of the Blood of Christ. There exists a degree of similarity in probabilities.

The Rito del Padre (Creek of the Father or Priest) heads against the side of Cerro Chimayosos (Chimayo Peak), and joins the main Pecos at Beatty's Cabin. Its principal tributary is the Rito de los Chimayosos which joins it in a deep canyon a mile and a half above Beatty's. The Cerrito del Padre (Little Peak of the Father) is a little, aspen-crowned, grassy-sided peak on the ridge between the Rito del Padre and the Chimayosos and breaks off abruptly to the junction. The top of the Cerrito del Padre is an unexcelled spot from which to get a close-up view of the western portion of the upper Pecos basin, for it sits out right in the center of it.

How did this peak and creek get their names? What incident or activity could a priest have been involved in here in this remote area to warrant the names? The priests and missionaries of pioneer days certainly often left their marks and impressions upon the countryside in both fact and legend. There are plenty of legends which might well explain these unique, distinctive names, and there must be some facts to sustain the long-persistent legends.

Many stories have been told of how some Catholic priests once had a rich gold mine in the Rito del Padre country. Burro loads of fabulously rich gold ore, it is said, were packed out to Mora on the east and Santa Fe on the west. If we knew that were so, then there would be no need to speculate further as to the source of the names. Usually, news of a gold strike spreads like wildfire, but for some reason, the location of this supposedly fabulous mine was kept a dark secret. Even unto death, no hint of the location of the mine was revealed to anyone.

Whether there ever was such a mine or not, perhaps no one will ever know, but, for years, the belief in it was persistent and first one party then another would go to the Pecos high country to look for the Padres' lost mine. Less than fifteen years ago, some prospectors called at my office to get whatever information I could give them about old prospect holes in the upper Pecos. They were planning a trip in search of the lost mine of the *padres*. Presumably, they, like all their treasure-hunting predecessors, found nothing for I never heard of them again.

I know of no concrete evidence that such a mine ever existed, but there can be little doubt that men of the cloth tried to find a mine there. In the 1850's, when the rich placer gold deposits were discovered at Elizabethtown, in a high valley between two mountain ranges, a hundred miles to the north, feverish prospecting activities became prevalent throughout the whole region. If gold were in one place, they reasoned, it must be in others and for years the mountains were combed in search of the glittering metal, love of which is the root of all evil.

Recently, while talking with a Catholic priest well versed in the history of the region, he said, "Most priests in the early days wanted to get rich and, when gold was discovered, they not only became interested but active." Some names of those who may have been active in the Pecos high country and got a creek and a peak named for them are Father Nicolas Valencia, 1845 to 1853, or, perhaps, Father Jovenceau, in the late 1850's, but more likely still, Father Tafoya, who was in the region from 1835 to 1860.

Father Tafoya is reported to have been very active and interested in mining as well as the salvation of souls. When he was moved to the village of Picacho, two hundred miles to the south, he had money to buy up some lands there. Then he met sudden and unexpected death by being thrown from a horse. If Father Tafoya had a mine, the secret of its location was buried with him.

Perhaps, it was not Father Tafoya at all but others who came after him. Despite the fact that no one else has ever found gold or other precious metals in the real Pecos high country, the legend of the Mine of the Fathers still persists. One thing seems certain; some *padre* must have carried on some activity there. How else would the Rito del Padre and Cerrito del Padre have gotten their unique names?

There is another story which, in some respects, seems more plausible than the gold mine legend. I was told by old timers years ago that, during the period beginning in the late 1860's, when sheep were first taken to the high country to graze for brief periods in summer, certain priests would go up there to say mass for the herders. In those days there had to be several herders with each band of sheep to keep the herds from getting all mixed up. Today, wherever sheep graze on the national forests, the various bands are assigned to graze on individual or small community allotments, but in those days there was no national forest, and the whole country was a big open range where each band of sheep grazed wherever it pleased the *caporal* (camp boss) unless someone else beat him to it. In the vicinity of Cerrito del Padre was some of the choicest grazing country, and perhaps a score or more bands would congregate in the area, vying with each other for the best spots. Thus, with four or five herders to each band of five hundred to a thousand sheep, there would be quite a big group of souls to be looked after.

There is a nice grassy slope on the east and south sides of Cerrito del Padre, bordered below by dense clumps of spruce and fir trees. It is said that this spot was more than once selected for the religious ceremony. The Padre would send word in advance what day he would be there. A camp would be made at the edge of the meadows, on Rito del Padre a little way northeast of the peak. Then several herders, under the direction of one of the *caporals,* would cut small fir trees and branches and construct an arched bower under the shelter of a clump of big fir and spruce trees.

In farming communities, where mass is sometimes held out in the open, the womenfolk decorate the bower with lace, linen sheets, cut-out stars, Christmas tree trimmings and, sometimes, with personal jewelry. In the absence of such articles here in the high mountains, the bower would be decorated with neatly-arranged small aspen and willow branches, herbaceous vines and leaves, and such flowers as larkspur, blue columbines, gentians, asters, buttercups, king's crown, and others.

The altar would be made of small poles cut from aspen saplings, and decorated with evergreen branches and flowers. The priest would bring wax candles, vestments and altar wine. Due to the remoteness of the spot, a day's journey to the nearest settlement, the organ would have to be dispensed with. Altar boys and, perhaps, a little choir would be recruited from the sheep camps, for often young boys were taken into the mountains to tend camp. When the herders and *caporals* assembled, they would bring whatever little santos, bultos, rosaries, and holy pictures they might have and, surprisingly enough, some of these articles usually would be found in every camp.

One herder would be left with each band of sheep and all the others would gather at the appointed place, some of them traveling several mountain miles afoot or burro-back. The priest would have come to the nearby camp on the previous day. The herders would form a procession, carrying the banner of Our Lady of Guadalupe and singing Spanish hymns, and march around the side of the peak to the altar. If there were any penitents among the herders, and in those days there always were, they would head the procession and direct it.

After mass, all would go to the camp, where a steaming hot meal of *chili con came, tortillas,* and black coffee would be served. After the feast was over many of the herdsmen would hurry back to their respective herds to relieve those who had been left to attend the sheep so that they could come for a late afternoon mass to be said for them, also.

I like to think this is how the Cerrito del Padre and the Rito del Padre got their names, rather than through the gold mine theory. It fits better in this divinely-favored setting. Yet there was some resemblance to the gold mine, for the next day the owners or *caporals* of the various bands would bring together the *"premisa"* or offering, not in a collection plate but on the hoof, and the priest, aided by his servants, would set out for home with a nice little band of sheep all his own.

Penitente Peak, undoubtedly, got its name from the use made of it by *Los Penitentes*, a vanishing religious order or brotherhood, whose members practiced self torture to atone for their sins. It is said that pilgrimages to the top of the peak were sometimes made by the more zealous of the penitent ones, carrying heavy crosses. Though unenlightened and unorthodox to our way of belief and worship, there is a bold lesson in devotion, and courage of one's convictions.

Rito del Perro is just plain Dog Creek and no one seems to care how it got its name. Palocientos is a picturesque name well illustrative of the place; palo is log or timber, cientos is hundreds. The place called Palocientos is an area where, as a result of an old burn, there are hundreds of logs lying crisscrossed and entangled.

Rio de la Casa is simply the River of the House, maybe originally Rio de la Caza, River of the Hunt, misspelled. Rito del Macho is Mule Creek. Rito Chaparrito (or Chaperito, as some maps have it, meaning an inclined plain descriptive of the area at the head of the creek) is Little Brush Creek. Rincón Bonito, one fork of the Rio de la Casa, is Pretty Cove; and if you doubt that it lives up to its name, a glimpse of it from the Rio La Casa—Pecos Divide—will convince you. Then there is Laguna Encantada, Enchanted Lake, nestling up to the east face of the Main Range.

Panchuela, name of an important creek and the ranger station on it, from which the Pecos high country is managed, cannot be found in the dictionary. Locally, it seems to mean a piece of flat, open country fanning out from a timbered area. Possibly, it is derived from the word "poncho" meaning a military coat. The description given first fits the mouth of Panchuela Creek. Some years ago, the U. S. Forest Service renamed the Panchuela Ranger Station "Overton W. Price" for the great early-day organizer of the Forest Service under Giffort Pinchot. But the name didn't stick. Panchuela, whatever it might mean, had too firm a foundation.

My old lion hunting friend, S. L. Fisher, who probably would not have recognized the name in print, always referred to the place as the "Bunch o' Willers." That would fit, too, I know, for a bucking bronco threw me higher than a kite there one day and I landed on my head right in a bunch of willows.

14

we hunt
the elk

When elk were restocked in the Pecos high country there were three objectives: To restore to the wilderness that which man had ruthlessly destroyed; to establish this lordly game for sport hunting; and to increase the wild meat supply. For a number of years after the release of thirty-seven head of elk, in 1915, the objectives seemed slow of realization. The slow start may be attributed to the poor, tick-infested condition of the animals when released and to subsequent poaching.

By 1933, the herd probably numbered about 300 head, although some-estimated it as low as 200, and a few overly-optimistic ones as high as 2,500. At that time the State Game Commission decided a limited and restricted season would be consistent with good game management. Elk being highly polygamous, the taking of a few bulls could not impair the breeding potential of the herd. It was felt that hunting seasons for bulls with at least three tines on each antler would be proper to start with, and that such a season would greatly stimulate public interest in the protection of the herd.

When the first season was announced, there were vociferous protests from some sportsmen and sportsmen's organizations. "It will be just like shooting a cow, no sport to it at all," angrily asserted the president of the State Game Protective Association. "It will mean the complete destruction of the herd." But the Game Commission felt it was right and went ahead, despite the protests. At the end of the ten-day season, only three bull elk had been taken by the ninety-seven hunters, and some sportsmen admitted they simply didn't know their elk or the Pecos high country either. Thereafter, for several years, there were not nearly enough applicants to take up the one hundred permits offered.

The seasons were continued and the kill gradually increased. As the herd kept on building up, the standards were lowered until, for several years, it was legal to take elk of either sex and any age. Good management requires that the elk herd be kept under control to prevent undue competition with livestock in the use of the public range, for which there is great demand; however, the demand for elk-hunting permits is very great, also, being two or three times the number of permits which can properly be issued. To pass the privilege around, the hunter who has a permit one year is not eligible to receive a permit the next.

In 1951, 150 hunters, selected by a public drawing from applicants, participated in this thrilling sport. Seventy hunters bagged elk and brought back over twenty thousand pounds of savory wild meat, and hides enough for seven hundred pairs of the finest gloves. Of greater value is the recreational relief from the claustrophobia of office strain and other confining occupations. The most intense enjoyment, no doubt, accrues to those who have the hardihood to pack in to the interior of the wilderness to do their hunting.

Whether I have a permit or not, I pack into the Pecos high country, with a few congenial companions, and spend a week during elk season, where the sound of running water is a substitute for the ringing telephone, and the pungent aroma of the forest replaces the smell of gasoline.

Perhaps it will not be amiss to tell about some of the many exciting, unusual elk hunts in the Beatty's Cabin country, with which I have been connected in one way or another during the past eighteen years.

Although I had killed several elk at Vermejo Park, it was the fall of 1934 that I had my first elk hunt in the Pecos. With fresh memories of the game depredations of the previous year at the outlaw cabin, Ranger J. W. Johnson, Deputy Game Warden Homer Pickens, and I decided we would patrol that area personally and put a stop to any similar activities before they got started. Ranger Johnson packed into Beatty's Cabin on October 24, but Homer and I were delayed and spent that night at Cowles with Skipper Viles.

We were not far behind though, for Skipper got us up at three o'clock and, by four, while it was still pitch dark, we were in the saddles, leading our two pack horses, on the trail to Round Mountain. We arrived at

Beatty's a few minutes after seven to find that Johnson had already left on patrol. We knew he would head for the outlaw cabin so we separated and spent the day on patrol in other areas. While our primary job was to supervise the elk hunters and patrol for violations, I had taken an elk permit and fully intended to get a big bull elk. In our patrols, we saw quite a lot of elk sign, and I noted in particular the huge track of a monstrous bull which was ranging nearby, first in the east, then in the west Beatty's Park areas. I wanted that bull.

One day while on patrol up at the outlaw cabin, I rode Prince, a big, stout mountain horse, around the hillside toward the Santa Barbara trail at the head of the river. Suddenly Prince threw up his head and, with ears thrown forward, gazed intently toward the timber across the park. At first, I could neither see nor hear anything. Pretty soon a chickaree squirrel began to chatter and I knew something had disturbed him. Then I glimpsed three nice mule deer bucks heading for the opening where the Santa Barbara trail crosses.

I touched spurs to Prince's sides and loped him to a spot where I could see the opening the bucks would have to cross. They soon came out of the timber and stopped about 175 yards away, presenting a perfect chance for a clean kill. While I did not especially want a deer, the chance tempted me and, since I can resist everything but temptation, I pulled my rifle from the scabbard, stepped off the horse, drew bead on the ten-point buck in the lead, and squeezed the trigger. At the crack of the rifle the big buck kicked with both hind feet—a sure sign he was badly hit—and started forward. A second shot went over his back, hitting the bank beyond. The big fellow turned and ran swiftly straight downhill for sixty paces, collapsed, and rolled over dead, the bullet having passed through his heart. I quickly dressed him and hung him in a tree by pulling him up with a rope to the saddle horn. I then cut spruce branches and draped them over him to protect the meat from ravens and Canadian jays.

I hunted elk all the way back but all I found was tracks and droppings where a little bunch had been here, and a lone bull there, in canyons and parks. At camp, I found that Homer had killed a nice young buck early that morning and I could not boast of getting first meat. All the same, we had a dandy supper of liver and bacon, French fried potatoes, and hot biscuits.

Next day, up at 3:00 A.M. and a long ways from the cabin by daylight, we patrolled and I hunted some. Again I saw the tracks of the big bull but that was all. Homer and Johnson "just happened" to pass by where I had killed my deer and packed it in for me on one of their saddle horses, taking turns walking and riding the other. That's the kind of guys they are.

We had all gotten in early that day and, after a three o'clock dinner, I went out afoot to the east Beatty's Park in quest of the big old bull. I guessed wrong for he was not there. Instead, just before sundown, I spied five elk in the west Beatty's Park, across the canyon over a mile away. One of the elk was very white sided and much larger than the others. That much could be seen with the naked eye. Quickly, I focused my 6x30 binoculars on the scene and what a sight it was! I had no doubt that was the big bull. He was magnificent and twice the size of the four cows with him. His antlers, though dimly outlined in the evening light, were, without doubt, a huge rack. It was too late to get to him before sundown when the legal shooting hour stops, so I went back to camp, bemoaning my bad judgment in going to the wrong park. At camp we decided the chances were good for the big bull and the four cows to bed down in the park during the night, as is their habit, and linger until sunrise to get their breakfast.

Next morning before it was light enough to shoot, Homer and I tied our horses in the thick timber below the park where the bull had been seen, and silently crept to the edge of the grassy opening. Right on the legal dot, which then was a half-hour before sunrise, we saw movement in the corner of the park above us. Training the binoculars on the spot, we could see two cows, three cows, four cows, all feeding as they slowly traveled toward the timber, but no bull. Satisfied he wasn't there, we searched the whole park with the glasses but he was nowhere to be seen. We got our horses and rode across the big opening, searching those spots which could not be seen from our stand, but no bull. We came back and examined the tracks where the cows had gone into the timber and, sure enough, the big old fellow had led them in, getting himself under cover of the forest before it was either light enough or 'legal to shoot.

We waited for a while, giving the elk time to bed down for the day, and then followed the tracks into the dry, noisy forest, entangled with windfalls which made travel difficult. In about a half-mile, we jumped the elk from their well-hidden beds. We failed to see them but heard the big bull go crashing through the timber. We returned to camp greatly disappointed. Homer returned to Cowles that afternoon but I could stay one more day and Johnson would stay until the season was over. I determined to get a bull elk that afternoon or next day, even if I didn't get the big one.

After dinner I asked Johnson to go with me but he wanted to paint the cabin roof, so I set out on Prince to cover as much country as I could before dark. I figured that, if I covered enough parks and glades, eventually I would surprise an elk in one of them. I rode up to the head of Cebadilloso Creek, where at least too good bulls had been ranging. From there, I went over to the south fork of the Azul where more elk had been ranging, then on around to the north fork of Rito Azul. It was the same story—plenty of tracks and marbles but no elk, not even a cow. It was getting late, so I hurried down the Azul to the Chimayosos and down it to the Rito del Padre. The steep, grassy slopes and bench lands west of the Padre are excellent elk feeding grounds and the elk should have been out. The sun had left the canyons and was just touching the ridge tops and peaks. "You will have to hurry and show yourself, Mr. Elk, if you are to save the Game Warden's reputation," I thought, as I rounded a clump of trees on an open bench near an old sheep corral. Suddenly, not twenty paces away, two bulls scurried from behind some aspens, then stopped right out in the open. I jerked my rifle from the scabbard but, damn it, they were both yearlings—dinky spike bulls—and it took three points on a side to be legal. For an instant hope dropped to zero. Legal hours would be over at sundown, and Elk Mountain, the highest peak in sight, was the only one still red with the glow of the setting sun. "Hello, there!" Three more bulls a hundred yards away—two legal three-year-olds and their "granddad." Rifle in hand, I fell off Prince, hastily drew bead on the big bull as he ran directly away from me, hoping to break the pelvis bone since the rump was all I could see to shoot at.

At the crack of the rifle, he turned to the right and started downhill broadside to me, shaking his head from side to side as he ran. What a shot this was! I couldn't miss and I didn't. The big fellow went down in a heap with a broken neck. The first bullet had grazed his hip and shoulder and hit the point of the left jaw, breaking it to pieces and turning him around for the coup de grace. He was a dandy specimen; the heavy, twelve-point antlers, with a spread of forty-three inches and forty-seven inch length, were even and beautifully ivory tipped. It was an elk to be proud of, and I am still proud of the mounted trophy looking down on me as this is written, but he was not the really big elk that I had so much wanted. I dressed him, turned him up on his belly to drain and cool out and rode to Beatty's in the pitch dark. Johnson had heard the shots from his painting perch on the roof and was not surprised that I had made a kill. I do believe, though, he was as happy as I was that I had gotten my elk.

Next day the job of skinning and quartering the big fellow and packing out the five hundred pounds of meat proved to be more work than fun.

Back at Santa Fe, I found that Ellis Bauer, Dick Healy, and Fletcher Catron were planning to leave next day for Beatty's Cabin to try for elk during the last days of the season. I told Ellis about the big old bull and that it was likely he would be back in the east Beatty Park after having been disturbed at the west park. Ellis, being an excellent hunter and sportsman, was eager to try for that remarkable animal.

Next day was blustery and snowing a little in the high country, affording a tracking snow. The party packed in over Hamilton Mesa, and Dick and Fletcher went on in to camp, while Ellis turned off the trail on a bench where a dim path leads to the east Beatty Park. Soon, he saw some dim, snow-filled tracks and followed them anxiously. A quarter-mile farther on, he came upon the fresh beds of a nice herd of elk and, sure enough, there was the huge track I had told him about.

The elk had, only a short while before, gotten up and were heading toward the east Beatty Park. It was a dark, blustery afternoon, ideal for hunting. Ellis, tingling all over with excitement and anticipation of a shot at the big boy, quickly tied up his horse, and afoot, followed the fresh tracks, which were pointing toward the east Beatty Park. The snow condition made it possible to travel very quietly through the forest, but the wind was not in his favor and he realized that it might carry man scent to the herd ahead of him, although there was not much he could do about it.

At the willowy fringe of the park, he saw a cow and a calf feeding. They had not seen or smelled him. He froze in his tracks until they went out of sight into the dense willows, then he hurried forward and went around the point of willows to where he could see up through the main opening, and there they were, a band of twenty or more elk scattered over the park, where they had been feeding.

At sight of the intruder, they threw up their heads and some of the wise old cows started off. Some of the younger ones hesitated briefly to stare at the hunter, who was looking for the big bull. Then a nice bull trotted out from behind some bushes. It was a dandy, but still it didn't look big enough to fit the tracks, but that must be he, no other bull was around. "I'd better take him," Ellis thought, slipping the safety off his .300 Savage rifle and raising it to shoot. "Wait a minute!" and he checked himself just in time.

There was a big movement in the edge of the willows and a second bull started out across the opening in the direction the cows had gone. What a magnificent bull it was! There was no doubt about his lordship being the coveted big one. There was little time for a shot as the bull ran full speed, angling across the neck of the park, toward cover. Quickly the ready rifle was trained on the prize target, and the big bull went down in a heap and lay still. Ellis rushed over near him, ready for another shot, expecting the huge animal to get up, but it wasn't necessary. While he had aimed for the heart, the bullet caught the bull in the back of the head, killing him instantly.

The quartered meat weighed 622 pounds, the hide and head, with antlers, weighed 138 pounds, and 20 pounds of neck meat was thrown away, which means the animal hog-dressed 780 pounds. Doubt it? O. K.., just drop in and see the trophy in Ellis Bauer's den some day and you will be convinced. It is the most magnificent elk trophy I have ever seen: 49 1/2-inch spread, 57 1/2-inch length, 13 points, beams measuring 12 1/2 inches in circumference at the burr, and 17-inch brow tines. It's in the record book.

After removing the entrails, Ellis went back to his horse and rode into camp, as though he were carrying the mail, to report an accomplishment of a lifetime to his hunting partners. I have known Ellis Bauer for many years and have never seen him under the influence of liquor, yet it is reported that he celebrated that evening, and far into the night, on the quart of Scotch which had been brought along for an occasional evening toddy. Who can blame him? Most fellows would have heart failure if they should kill an elk like that one.

A CHALLENGE

To prevent undue congregation of hunters in any single area, the Department of Game and Fish reserves the right to assign hunters to their respective camp sites, giving consideration to their wishes as much as possible. One year I assigned a group of three hunters to the Horse Thief Meadows, where I knew some elk were coming in to feed. They camped right out in the middle of the area; and, no doubt, the wood chopping and other camp activity, campfire and smoke, buggered the elk, for the hunters failed to find any. Naturally, they blamed me and were sore because they didn't get an elk. They challenged me to go there the next year and, just for the hell of it, I agreed, and bet them I would get an elk.

Dick Healy, Charlie Miller, and Ellis Bauer, my hunting partners that year, packed in the day before the season opened, made camp out of sight down by the creek, and prepared for a daylight start on opening day. I was, as usual, delayed and left Santa Fe at 3:00 A.M. I drove to Cowles, where I picked up a saddle and pack horse, and rode on in to camp at Horse Thief Meadows, as I had agreed. I got there about eight o'clock, and, of course, the others were already out hunting. I unpacked, Hobbled my pack horse, and set out to find where elk were ranging and bedding. Up toward the head of the Panchuela the timber is not too dense but it is a favorite place for elk to go to bed down when they have been undisturbed. If disturbed they seek a brushy and loggy retreat to make their day beds.

I had never ridden that horse before and had no idea what he would do if a shot was fired off of him or near him. I began seeing some sign, tracks, droppings, and an occasional bed or two where the dwarf huckleberry bushes had been mashed down. I was traveling slowly, not expecting to see any game, and had my .32 Winchester Special in a scabbard.

Both the horse and I were startled when two three-year-old bull elk jumped up out of their beds 150 feet away. One was directly in front of me and he took off to my left like the devil was after him. The other was to my right and he just stood there broadside, partially screened by some small fir trees. The horse had stopped, head held high, at sight of the elk. I slowly wrapped the bridle reins around the horn of the saddle several times, eased the rifle out of the scabbard, and, as I shoot left-handed, turned slightly to the right in the saddle in position to shoot. As quietly as I could, I levered a cartridge into the chamber and, carefully avoiding any quick move, I raised the rifle, took deliberate aim for the place where the elk's heart ought to be, and, disregarding what the horse might do, squeezed the trigger. The horse jumped about ten feet, snorted and tried to buck, but the reins were too tight to the saddle horn.

Out of the corner of my eye, I had seen the elk take off at top speed back the way I had come. The pony was soon quieted and I rode over to where the bull had been standing and noted a tuft of hair cut off by the bullet, but no blood. It was just too close a shot to miss, even though the breathing of the horse made it hard to hold a steady bead. Maybe I had only wounded him, so I tied up the horse and followed the tracks afoot, but could see no blood. Then I came upon him stone dead, shot squarely through the heart. He had run a hundred and seventeen yards from a standing start, and spilled no blood along the way. Never should one think he has missed an elk just because he doesn't go down; follow on, until you are sure, one way or another.

The others were unlucky that year and didn't get an elk.

One evening when Bauer, Miller, and I got into camp, we saw Dick Healy sitting by a little fire of his own a hundred feet away from camp and talking to himself. "What's wrong, Dick?" we called, but no answer. We went over to him but he still wouldn't talk except to use a certain amount of profanity with reference to his luck, his rifle, and his ammunition. He was the maddest man I ever saw. We went on to camp, built a fire, and soon had a pot of coffee boiling. We started supper, wondering all the while what was eating on Dick. Charlie Miller took a cup of hot coffee over to him, persuaded him to drink it, and he finally came on over and joined us at camp. But not until after supper did we get this story out of him.

While hunting near the head of Panchuela, he had sat down near a big, dead log at the lower edge of an open glade. Soon he heard a noise back of him, looked around, and, to his amazement, there stood a huge brown bear. The big fellow was fat, the fur long and shiny. One never could hope for a better shot. Quickly, Dick took perfect bead for the region of the heart and squeezed the trigger. The .300 Savage just snapped. He quickly injected another cartridge in the chamber and, as Bruin was leaving there, took aim. The rifle misfired again. A third time he levered a cartridge in and still had time for perfect aim at the bear galloping across the glade, but, as before, the rifle snapped. Then the bear was gone.

What was it? It had never happened to him before. Bad ammunition? Something wrong with the firing pin? Or just jinxed? He didn't know. No wonder he was provoked. Actually, bad ammunition was the answer.

That ended our hunting trip. I was sorry my companions had been unsuccessful, but there was a degree of satisfaction in reporting to the disgruntled hunters of the previous year that I had gone to Horse Thief Meadows as agreed, and had gotten a three-year-old bull elk, where they had failed.

Playing Guide

To me, it has been a greater pleasure to help others get a shot at an elk than to kill one myself. Maybe it's because, in that way, one gets the thrill and fun of hunting, tracking, and stalking the quarry without the responsibility of dressing, skinning, quartering, and packing out the meat and trophy. But I usually wind up doing a lot of that work, too.

Once I visited a camp of hunters which Frank Means had taken to the mouth of Rito de los Esteros. They had had no luck, were discouraged and disappointed with the hunt, and planned to pack out next morning. I spent the night with them and persuaded them to stay until noon next day, promising I would do my best to get one of them a shot next morning. It was agreed, and a man by the name of Gregg was chosen to go with me.

At daylight we rode up a dim trail through the tangled forest toward the parks on Rito Las Trampas. There was a little wet snow in the timber but none in the open. Near the top, we hit the track of a big, lone bull elk and followed it to the first park. There, in the little grassy area, he had fed the evening before, bedded down for the night, then made his breakfast there. He had gone back into the timber downhill toward the Mora River. He had been gone only a few minutes and I was sure we could overtake him, but it seemed wise to wait an hour or so to give the old fellow a chance to get bedded down for the day. Meanwhile, we scouted a few other parks but found nothing.

We tied up the horses and set out afoot on the track of the big bull. Gregg remarked that had he been alone, he never would have found where the bull had left the little park. I told him I would do all the trailing and looking for the elk and for him to spend all his time being quiet and staying close behind me. We took it very slowly and quietly and, in about a quarter of a mile, I raised up from a crouching position to look over the tops of a clump of little spruce saplings, and there he was in his bed 150 feet down the hill. He was broadside to us, chin stretched out on the ground, sound asleep.

I eased back down out of sight, motioned for my hunter to keep low and come to me quietly. Whispering very softly, I told him what I had seen, what to do, where to aim, and cautioned him to be sure he held dead on the target. Then I let him raise up very slowly just enough to see over the bushes and shoot. I saw where the bullet hit right behind the shoulder, just a trifle high but I knew it was a fatal shot. The big bull jumped to his feet and ran around the hillside for sixty or seventy yards and stopped. Gregg shot several more times but by then he had the buck ague too bad to hit anything.

Soon the big bull staggered and fell over. We rushed over there and I got ready to stick him. Thinking he was down for keeps, we both had set our rifles down against a tree a few feet away. When I plunged my hunting knife in his neck, just above the brisket, pointing straight for the heart, the big twelve-point bull jumped to his feet. I sprang back out of the way and stayed safely behind a tree. Gregg grabbed an antler and held on like a cowboy bulldogging a steer. I yelled at him to get the hell away from there before he got a tine run through him. But he held on, retorting that "I'll be damned if I am going to let him get away."

I was scared stiff he would get hurt badly, as the bull threw him around first one way, then the other, but I knew that both the bullet and knife wound were fatal. After a half-minute packed chockfull of action, the old bull went down for good and the bulldogger had miraculously escaped injury: The bullet had passed just over the heart and he should never have gotten up, but an elk is tough and tenacious of life and can carry a lot of lead. Gregg and his party were just as happy and grateful as could be, and my reputation as a guide gained some staunch champions.

On another occasion, a bunch of us were camped in the little Forest Service cabin at Beatty's, and two of the fellows, Ira Sefton and Lamar Lamb, had had no luck. They each wanted a bull and I offered my services as a guide. It was our custom to get up at 3:30 or 4:00 A.M. to start wrangling horses, getting breakfast, and putting up noon lunches, so we could reach wherever we wanted to be by legal time to start shooting.

On this particular morning at 4:00 o'clock, it was snowing and blowing and it was cold enough to frost the ears of a brass monkey, so we decided to lie abed awhile. About daylight we got up and it quit snowing. We were sorry then that we hadn't gotten out earlier. We hurried around and I told Sefton and Lamb I felt sure we could find them a bull apiece. They were dubious, but the four-inch new snow was ideal for trailing and they gladly accepted my proffered services as a guide.

Up near Jaroso Creek, we hit the tracks of two bulls—just what we wanted. Had we been there at daylight, as we should have been, we would have caught them out in the parks just right. We followed a little way on horseback; then, as it seemed they were only a short distance ahead, we tied up the horses and took it afoot. Soon it began to snow again and the rifles and our gloves got wet, but we stayed right on the tracks.

Finally, the tracks crossed the Pecos below Jaroso Creek and headed into the deep timber south of the river. Despite the lateness of the hour, the bulls continued to feed some as they traveled around the hillside. They would stop in the timber as if going to lie down, then change their minds and go on to the next glade and nuzzle down in the snow for herbs and grass. It was evident that we were very close to them, and we watched ahead through the timber carefully, and traveled as quietly as possible.

One of the bulls was a particularly big one, and we knew he had an exceptionally big rack because he wouldn't attempt to go between two trees that were closer than four feet apart, and he knocked snow off of branches eight feet high. He intrigued us with the many evidences of his size and lordliness.

We entered a little glade on their tracks. I was in front and Lamar was right back of me, while Sefton was thirty feet below and a little farther back. There was a big spruce tree in the glade just below and in front of

Sefton. When we got out into the glade, I squatted down to look under the branches of the trees beyond. Then I noticed the big track had turned straight down the hill through the middle of the glade, while the other had gone straight on across it. I looked to my right, down the way the track had gone, but could see nothing. I eased forward a few steps, squatted, and looked again.

There he was in all his magnificence. He had been behind the big tree and now Lamar and I had come around it, and the big fellow was in plain sight only two hundred feet away. The tree still hid him from Sefton. The bull didn't see us as he nuzzled down in the snow at the base of a bushy little spruce for food. I motioned slowly to Lamar, but he had just seen the bull and was standing quietly in shooting position. Suddenly, he jerked his gloves off and started fooling with the .300 Savage rifle. Just as suddenly, the bull saw the quick movement and threw up his head to stare unbelievingly at us for a brief second. I had my rifle and could easily have shot him, but I had already killed my elk. I didn't know what was wrong. Why didn't Lamar shoot? He would never have another chance at a glorious bull like that again.

Before I could find out what was wrong and offer my rifle, the big lordly animal turned and dashed out of sight in the forest. Lamar was shaking with excitement. "What the hell, why didn't you shoot?" I asked.

"I couldn't get the safety off."

On the Savage rifle there is a little slot where the safety lever slides forward and back. The snow had gotten packed in the slot and froze solidly, locking the little lever on safety. All that work for nothing, and our chances ruined by a sliver of ice a half-inch long. Years ago, when I worked at times as a professional guide, I would have had to laugh that sort of thing off and enthusiastically set out on the trail again to make another opportunity. It's different when you are guiding for fun.

We did follow on for a little way, then I turned back, for once bulls have been spooked, it's a long hard trail to get to them again. Sefton and Lamar went on and jumped them once more but did not see them. Then they turned the tracks over to another hunter and he had a try with no better success.

A few years ago, I was returning from an early morning ride which I had made from Beatty's Cabin up into the Azul and down the Cebadilloso when, at about ten in the forenoon, I encountered a novice elk hunter in a grassy park gazing longingly at elk tracks, beds, and piles of droppings where the elk had been at daylight. He looked as if he thought the elk should still be there. I told him they were accustomed to take cover in the deep forest during daytime, then showed him where they had left the park that morning.

"How far is it to their bed grounds?" he asked.

"From a half-mile to a mile back in the forest."

"Do you think I could find them?"

"Tell you what, you leave your horse here, and follow that dim path the tracks start out on, go very slow and absolutely quiet, away back in the deep forest. Look sharp and you might get one."

"Thanks, I'll try it."

I rode on in to camp and a few hours later the hunter came in bloody from gutting an elk.

"Well, good, you got one, I see," I greeted him.

"Sure did, it was easy."

"Tell me about it," I said, for I had thought he hadn't much chance since he was unfamiliar with elk hunting.

"Well, I started like you told me," he said, "then I got scared I would not be able to find my horse again so I came back and got the horse and rode into the forest the way you said to go. It was pretty brushy and the horse made a lot of noise jumping logs and breaking limbs, and I was sure he would scare all the elk within a mile. Then the horse acted like he heard or saw something ahead, and he whinnied. Next thing I knew here came an old cow elk right toward me. I got off and got my rifle ready and, by that time, the cow was within fifteen feet of me, so I let her have it. It was easy, now I know how to hunt elk. Thanks a lot for telling me where to go."

"You're welcome," I said. What else was there for an old elk hunter who thought he knew all the answers to say?

HELPING EACH OTHER

Far too often one hunter helps another by killing his game for him. That's not legal, it's not orthodox, it's not sportsmanship. How any hunter can get pleasure or satisfaction out of having someone else kill his game for him, it is hard to understand. Personally, I would get just as much enjoyment out of having some other fellow do my kissing for me as I would for him to kill my game for me. No kiddin.

On the other hand, it is a great source of enjoyment to go along with a good hunting companion and back him up or have him go along with me, as the case may be. I have enjoyed hunting elk with many good fellows in the Pecos high country. Once, a few years ago, I was up at Beatty's but had no elk license. Kay Flock, forest supervisor, was up there on his first elk hunt in New Mexico. The first two or three days he failed to get an elk, and during that time I had been out with others with varying success.

One evening I kiddingly said, "If you will go with me in the morning, I'll show you plenty of elk."

"It's a deal; will you guarantee I get one?"

"No, but I'll guarantee you get a shot."

"Fair enough, for if I get a shot, I'll get an elk."

Next morning, Kay and I and, I believe, Don Clauser and Art Shilling, started out up the trail toward Jaroso. This trail follows a big bench half way up the mountain and passes through some excellent elk feeding parks. Just before we got to the first one where we might expect to see elk, we checked the time and it was just a minute before legal time to shoot. It would take about a minute to get to the edge of the big flat open park, so we rode on.

When we rode out from behind the last clump of trees, right there ahead of us was a nice bunch of elk, eight or ten of them. We got off and Kay fired at one, but since he was shooting right toward the east, the light was not good and he missed. The elk strung out in high gear across the park in front of us. Kay fired again and missed, and a third time and missed. By then they were pretty well around to the northwest which gave a much better light. Just as the two-year-old heifer he had been shooting at entered the aspen timber some 275 yards away, Kay fired again but the heifer went on out of sight.

"Well, that's that," he said disgustedly.

"Let's ride over there; it looked to me as if you might have got her that last shot," I said.

"Think so? No, I never touched her. I should have dropped her the first shot. The last one was too far."

"Always go look," I said, but I knew Kay would do that anyway just to be sure.

We rode over there, took the tracks where she entered the aspen, and, seventy yards farther on, there she lay stone dead with a bullet through her heart. Kay didn't say it but admitted his first thought was, "I wonder who killed that elk." What he did say a moment later was, "Well, I'll be damned."

"It's all in having a good guide," I said, with a straight face.

"That's right and I'll back you up next year for then you'll have a permit and I won't," Kay said.

"And that will suit me fine."

When the next season rolled around, it found Kay and me, Bob Ground, J. O. and John McCauley and others right back at Beatty's. The first morning, Kay and I went up to Beatty's Park and buggered some elk out but didn't get a shot. We started to follow them into the timber. I suggested we let them go and pick one up in the head of Cebadilloso Canyon that evening, for they were headed that way.

At a half-hour before time to quit shooting, we tied our horses back in the big island of timber in the head of the Cebadilloso and sat down by some bushes, where we could see across the strip of open area at the south side of the canyon head. It was cold as all get out, and we were bundled up in fur-collared, eider down coats. We spread down our chaps to sit on. We snoozed a little. Then, as time approached for the elk to come out—about ten minutes before sundown—we woke up and began an intense vigil.

"Time they were showing up," Kay whispered.

"Yep, it won't be long now," and in half a minute a cow walked out of the timber into the opening. "Want her?" Kay asked in a whisper.

"Nope, I want a yearling bull."

"Choosy, eh?"

"Yep, besides being top quality, it has volume, too."

Then a calf walked out. "Want it? It's tender."

"Nope, a spike bull will be next."

No sooner had I whispered that prediction than out walked a bull with 22-inch spikes—just exactly what I wanted—and he definitely was mine for he was only seventy yards away. I had my new .270 Winchester with K 2.5 scope, and it was to be my first elk with it. I fired for the heart, but the shot went two or three inches high. The bull swayed but didn't go down. I fired for his neck but, being entirely unused to the scope, I missed. Before I could fire again, he went down. When we got to him, he tried to get up and I gave him a mercy shot in the head.

The choice of location, the timing, and selection of the desired class of animal wanted were perfect in every respect. Too easy that time, but thoroughly enjoyable by reason of being backed up by a swell hunting partner. •

Another instance of perfect timing was one season when Ranger J. W. Johnson couldn't get away from Panchuela Station on the day before the season opened. When we others left, he said, "I'll leave here early and get to the big Beatty Park by eight-thirty. That will be about time for some of the Round Mountain elk to be passing through after being shot into by the hunters down there."

At eight-thirty he rode out into the park and before he got through it a band of fifteen elk came across ahead of him, and he got a ten-point bull. He planned it that way.

A few years ago, we had a dandy party of good fellows camped at Beatty's after the Game Department's new administrative cabin was built. There were seven or eight of us in all, some had elk permits; some didn't. I was one who didn't and, as usual, I went out first with one hunter, then another, or alone on patrol. In the evening we sat around and told each other of the day's adventures, made plans for the morrow, and, occasionally, had a little penny ante game.

Angus Evans, member of the Game Commission, was there; also, Dr. Brubaker, Bill Stringfield, Dick Johnson, and several others. The first evening out Angus Evans' horse jumped a high log with him and severely bumped Angus' leg against a snag. The leg got awfully sore and Angus could hardly walk, but he refused to come to town until he got an elk. He had to hunt horseback all together and for several days had no luck at all. We begged him to come on in but, ardent hunter that he is, he determined to stay until he got an elk.

Finally, on the fifth day, four or five inches of snow fell. At noon, it let up and the sun came out through broken clouds. Conditions were ideal for elk hunting for if one could hit a track, it would have to be fresh and the elk could easily be trailed down. Since Angus would not agree to go home without an elk, and his leg was hurting and swelling worse all the time, I made up my mind I would get him a shot that afternoon or bust a cinch trying.

At two o'clock we set out for the big Beatty Park and, arriving a half-hour later, were elated to find that ten elk had been feeding there since it had quit snowing. It was certain they were close by and should be easy to get up to for a shot. Ordinarily, we would have followed the tracks on foot but, since Angus couldn't walk, we had to try it horseback.

Unfortunately, my hearing aid had gone out on me and I could hear hardly anything without it. That can get one into all kinds of predicaments. It has its advantages, also, as when some of the fellows start snoring or the alarm clock goes off. All the same, I determined to get Angus a shot at those elk. We followed the tracks into the edge of the scattered aspen and spruce timber. Then, as I peeked over a little rise, I could just see the heads of some elk which were lying down in the tall grass.

I motioned Angus to ride up beside me but his horse was not as tall as mine and he couldn't see a thing. He then got off and hobbled up even closer until he could see the back of a cow's head a hundred feet away. He shot at it and missed. I cussed at him for that, but couldn't hear what his alibi was. Meanwhile, elk got up all around us. I saw him work the bolt of his 30-06 to reload, but he made no attempt to shoot. "Shoot that one," I said. He looked at me, then at his gun, but I couldn't hear what he said.

Another elk stopped within a hundred feet of him. I lost patience and yelled, "Shoot that one, damn it!" He said something emphasized with a cuss word, took a cartridge out of his pocket and, apparently, put it in the magazine, worked the bolt, then instead of shooting an elk, said some bad words—I couldn't hear what. Still another elk passed within a few feet of him, but Angus just fooled with the rifle, while I cussed him out soundly. Soon the elk were all gone and he had frittered away his chance.

I rode over to where he was and he showed me what was wrong. The catch that holds the plate under the magazine had come loose and the cartridges had all fallen through into the snow. When he put another cartridge in, it went through, too. I was pretty peeved for never had I gotten a man better shots and I never so badly wanted a man to get his elk. We got the rifle fixed and then set out to find more elk, but I figured we had had our chance for the day. We spent an hour hunting the upper parks, but found nothing. Then, just before sundown, we came back down through this same big park. Angus was riding thirty yards back of me, when all of a sudden, I saw two bull elk feeding a hundred and fifty yards down the hill, at the edge of the aspens. One was a very fine, extra large bull with exceptionally high antlers, while the other was a two-year-old. I wanted Angus to have the big one for a trophy.

I turned and motioned for him to stop and he saw the smaller elk at once, but the big one was behind a tree from him and he couldn't see it. Hampered by his crippled leg, he literally fell off his horse in the snow, got up and started to shoot. I called to him, "Don't shoot, don't shoot, come down here, there's a big one." He pulled up his rifle anyway and again I called out, "Don't shoot, damn it all, don't shoot that one!"

Angus knew he could get that one and he hadn't seen the other, and said loud enough for the elk to hear him, even though I couldn't, "Awhile ago you cursed me for not shooting, now you tell me not to. You go to hell." I could read lips well enough to get that.

The bulls heard him and threw up their heads and Angus shot the two-year-old, knocking him down, but he got up and went behind the tree, where the big one had been and stopped. Meanwhile, the big high-antlered bull came out in sight, and when I looked at Angus, he had his rifle up and ready to shoot. I thought surely he was going to shoot the big one by mistake for the one he had wounded, and it just wouldn't do for the warden to have a commissioner on his hands with two elk. So again, I yelled. "Don't shoot, damn it, don't shoot, that's not the one you wounded." From the look he gave me, I wouldn't have been surprised if he had turned the gun on me. His lips seemed to frame the words, "Who the hell is doing this, anyway?" Angus held his fire and the tension eased when the big bull ran off, and the wounded one came out to receive another slug that Angus had waiting for him. Again the shot knocked him down, but he wouldn't stay down. I saw that he was mortally wounded and, as Angus raised his rifle, I said, for the steenth time, "Don't shoot." He didn't, but by the time the bull had gone three hundred yards down the hill before he lay down, I wished I had kept my mouth shut. It was plain the bull would die in a little while, but even so, he just might go on down into a rough canyon and give us a lot of trouble getting him out. I got Angus' horse for him, then rode quickly down to within 150 yards of the bull. By then he was threatening to get up. Angus was away behind because he could hardly ride down hill for his leg hurting. I called back to him, "Shall I give him the mercy shot for you?" He motioned for me to go ahead.

I squatted down and tried to break his neck. Three times I shot with my .32 Winchester special and three times the bull just shook his head. By then Angus was there, this time asking me sarcastically, "What the hell's the matter?"

"I can't figure it out," I said, "maybe you think you can do a better job."

"I sure can," he yelled, and he did. At the crack of the rifle, the bull's head dropped and it was all over. He would have died in a few minutes anyway as either of the first two shots was fatal. When we skinned him out, we found that all three of my bullets had gone through the neck just above the bone. One had gone clear through and the other two lodged against the skin on the opposite side. Such is the toughness of an elk's neck.

Back at camp I soon got my electric ear going again, and any misunderstandings that may have accrued between guide and hunter or warden and commissioner were quickly and completely dispelled.

There have been many other exciting, thrilling, disappointing, and satisfying experiences on deer and elk hunts in the Pecos high country, especially centering around Beatty's Cabin. Like the time my good friend,

Captain A. T. McDannald and three friends left Austin, Texas, one morning by plane, got to Santa Fe at 3:00 P.M., changed to cars and got to Cowles with me at 5:00 P.M., changed to horses and, after a terribly dark trail ride, got to Viles' Cabin a mile below Beatty's by 9:15 P.M., the same day. By seven-thirty next morning Cap had his bull elk.

I have camped at Beatty's and hunted with many fine fellows: Lee Wang, Ed Tucker, Dick Johnson, Art Schilling, Joe Rodriguez, Don Clauser, Frank Ortiz, J. O. and John McCauley, Les Langley, Wallace Wilson, Clarence Via, Wilbur McNeese, Kelly Kauffman, my son Roy, my brother Omar, A. B. Carpenter, Bob Ground, Speed Simmons, Marion Embrey, Ray Bell, Homer Pickens, and many others. There is a story or two about all of them, also, but they will have to wait until another time.

15

a miscellany of
short stories

The Last Grizzly

No story of the upper Pecos would be complete without a word about George A. (Skipper) Viles. In fact, the story of his interesting mountain life would fill a book all by itself. Mountain-raised, prospector of the Alaskan gold rush days, forest ranger, cattleman, and dude rancher, he had many a fine story to tell. The tragic part of it is that we all put off too long getting the material first hand—now it is too late.

Skipper Viles' father was an invalid and came to Willis, now Cowles, for his health in 1891, and bought the homestead at the junction of the Pecos River and Jack's Creek, which Joseph Blanger had settled on in 1888. Charles H. Viles' family consisted of his wife, his two sons, George A. and Harry C, and his daughter, Emma. Other early homesteaders on adjacent lands were Martin M. Winsor, where the Mountain View resort is now located and which Henry Winsor occupied for many years, and James H. Bullock, on Jack's Creek.

Charles H. Viles built the big one-and-a-half story house, with a fine fireplace, on the point between Jack's Creek and the Pecos. Later, this fine mountain dwelling was sold to some El Paso, Texas, people for a summer clubhouse. Years later, it was acquired by the owners of the Mountain View Ranch, and for a long time not much use was made of it. A tribute to those who built it is the fact that, in 1950, fifty-nine years after it was built, the old house was torn down, the heavy hewn logs, still absolutely solid, were marked to match, and it was rebuilt at the Mountain View Ranch headquarters.

Skipper Viles' father, suffering from tuberculosis, was being treated by Dr. Sparks, an old country doctor who doctored horses as well as people, and who lived at the east base of the Main Range where the Pecos-Rociada trail comes down, some fifteen miles away. While many cases of consumption, as it was then called, were greatly improved or entirely cured by the pure, invigorating air of New Mexico's mountains, Charles H. Viles, unfortunately, was not one of them. By 1894, he had become bedfast, but had great faith in Dr. Sparks' ability to cure him if only he could be under his constant care. Distance and topography prevented that unless he could be hospitalized at the Doctor's residence.

How to get the invalid over there was the big question. The thirty-mile trip by jolty wagon to the railroad, then by rail to Las Vegas, and another thirty-mile wagon trip to Dr. Sparks' home appeared to be more than he could endure. But pioneers had a way of getting things done despite obstacles, so a stout stretcher was improvised and a comfortable bed for Mr. Viles was made on it. Then four of his good neighbors, taking turn about, two at a time, carried the desperately-ill invalid on the stretcher all the way over the fifteen long miles by mountain trail across the rugged range to the Doctor's house. The trip was not only a unique performance but a valiant effort to save the man's life, deserving of reward. But it was in vain, for Charles H. Viles soon passed away at the Doctor's home.

Thus, Skipper Viles, at seventeen, for a time became the man of the house; however, his mother later married a man by the name of Hume and they moved to the east side of the mountain, and he built a hunting lodge in the Rincon Bonito, at the head of the Rio de la Casa. Skipper, Harry, and their sister, Emma, rode all over the Pecos high country and came to know it better than anybody.

Several years after the unsuccessful trip to Alaska in if with Tom Stewart, in search of gold, Skipper Viles became a forest ranger, as did his brother, Harry, and served for a time in that capacity. Then, in 1916 I believe it was, Skipper bought the property at Cowles, now known as the Mountain View Ranch, and operated it as a small cattle outfit and developed it into a summer resort, which, along with Skipper and Mrs. Viles, gained quite a widespread and favorable reputation.

Skipper Viles summer grazed his cattle in the Round Mountain and Beatty's Park area and built a two-room cabin a mile below Beatty's for the cowboys' summer headquarters. The cabin, recently torn down and replaced by a better one, has always been known as Viles' Cabin.

In 1923, I was operating a mountain ranch on Sapello Creek and summer grazing my cattle in the Beaver Creek and Big Burn country. A big grizzly bear came onto Skipper's range and killed some cattle. Skipper tried to trap him but the old bear was a smart one and had learned what traps were and refused to be caught. When he couldn't find a way to get to the carcass without getting caught, he would go kill another cow. I heard of all this and, although it was fifteen miles over there, I was on the lookout for him to come to my range and sample some of my beef.

Sure enough, one day I rode over to Beaver Creek and found he had been there and killed a two-year-old steer near the head of the north fork of Beaver, and a young cow three miles below, right near our branding corral. He had eaten a big meal out of the belly and rump of the first one, but the second he had just killed for fun. I thought he might come back so rode to the ranch and got some bear traps and a camp outfit so I could camp near the cattle. The Koogler boys, neighboring ranchers, came over and we set the traps. The old fellow didn't come back that night so the others went home. I took my three Airedales and tried to follow him, or, at least, find out which way he had gone and where he might strike next.

We found his big, foot-long track headed right down the dusty trail along Beaver Creek and followed it four miles to the junction with Hollinger Canyon. There he had turned right back up the Hollinger, sticking to the trail most of the way, his claw marks showing three inches ahead of the toe pads at every step. At the falls, five miles up the canyon, he turned out to the right and went up through the Big Burn to the top of the range. By then it was getting late and the track was still two days old, so I turned back and rode the eight long mountain miles back to the ranch.

That night I 'phoned Skipper Viles to be on the lookout for the grizzled old stock killer for he was headed back his way. Skipper reported that the bear had come back to one of his previous kills the night before and gotten caught in a trap waiting for his big foot, and that he had shot him that morning. That, as far as I know, was the last grizzly bear of the Pecos high country. From time to time, there have been reports of tracks of a grizzly being seen but certainly none lives there, and it could be only one occasionally passing through.

At the time I was a bit jealous of Skipper because he, not I, had killed the bear. Now, since it proved to be the last one, I am mighty glad I didn't kill it. Mrs. Viles still has the rug and it is really a nice one.

Skipper Viles was quite a character—unpredictable, self sufficient, distinctively opinionated, thrifty, honest but a shrewd trader, and endowed with a droll sense of humor. He had been quite a hunter and fisherman but slacked off in those activities in later years. Like most of the mountain folks of two or three decades ago, he had considered it an inalienable privilege to have a little wild meat occasionally, regardless of whether it was in season or out.

Not long before I became State Game Warden, in 1931, Skipper had gotten into a little difficulty with the law, over an out-of-season turkey, I think. I had known Skipper and his good wife for many years, so shortly after I took office, I drove out to have a little talk with him about the future welfare of game in the area.

"Skipper," I said, "I am going to ask you a direct question and I want a straight answer."

"Shoot; what is it?" was his quick reply.

"I want to know whether I am going to have to watch the game in this area or whether I can depend on your co-operation in protecting it."

He looked at me sharply for a few seconds, then gazed out across the canyon from where we sat on the commissary porch. For five minutes he mulled the question and all that it implied, over in his mind. I knew better than to crowd him. He shifted the cud of tobacco from one side of his mouth to the other and spat, narrowly missing a red ant dragging a beetle five times its size toward its nearby home. At last, he again looked at me steadily with piercing eyes, and said, "I have come to the conclusion that every deer, every turkey, and every bear is worth ten times more for my guests to see than their meat is on the table. I like to see it, too. Elliott, you can depend on me." Then, with a sly grin, he added, "It will be a good idea for my neighbors to lay off, too."

That was a promise that he lived up to until the day he died. That is the kind of man Skipper was.

THE GREAT FLOOD OF 1904

Chicago had its fire, San Francisco, its earthquake, and the Pecos high country, its flood. Indeed, the terrible deluge extended over all but the extreme western part of the territory of New Mexico. The previous winter had been one of exceedingly light snowfall and the spring and early summer saw very little rain, but September made up for it, and more.

The U. S. Weather Bureau report for September, 1904, has this to say, "Between the 26th and the 30th of September, very heavy steady rains fell over nearly the entire Territory causing the most extensive and destructive floods in its history. The greatest damage occurred on the 29th over the eastern slopes of the mountains and along the valleys of the Northern Portion." The nearest rain-gauging station to the Pecos high country was at Rociada, a few miles east of the Pecos headwaters. There the Weather Bureau records show that 7.92 inches of rain fell during the flood period, mostly in two days. No doubt more fell in the high country, for that is the usual precipitation pattern.

Again quoting from the U. S. Weather Bureau record, we find these statements picturing the fury of the deluge: "Past all imagination, conception or belief, say those who witnessed the spectacle, was the fury of the flood at the confluence of the Mora and Sapello Rivers." Speaking of two miles of Santa Fe railway tracks below Watrous, the report says, "The whole track was lifted bodily out of the long, narrow, winding box canyon and hurled two miles further down on the Shoemaker Ranch."

There is no record of the happenings in the Pecos high country other than the indelible marks left by the mad, raging, roaring waters. But today the evidence still remains for anyone to see. At the time, I was in school at Las Vegas and, three days after the rains ceased and the crest had passed, we had had no word from the folks at the ranch twenty-five miles away on Sapello Creek. I rented a horse at the livery barn and rode out to see if they were safe. Even on horseback, it was almost impossible to get there so badly washed out was the road. All were safe but several acres of rich farm lands had been carried away where the river had changed its winding course through the valley.

The Mora fork of the Pecos suffered greater damage than the main stream and its tributaries to the west. At that time, for the most part, there was a good ground cover of tall bunch grasses in the parks and open slopes and in such areas there was little damage done. On the other hand, wherever the rank vegetative ground cover had been impaired, the water was able to cut through the top soil and gouge out great gashes down the slopes. So great was the surface runoff that in some places on steep, aspen-covered slopes deep gullies were cut and trees uprooted and carried away; however, the most severe damage was done along the canyon bottoms, especially along the Mora, and from its junction with the main stream on down. In the canyon bottoms, regardless of willows, alders, and good ground cover, the immense accumulation of water from the supersaturated soil was so great that most of the fine meadows along the stream were washed out and replaced with great deposits of barren rubble and boulders. Here and there, in the narrower canyons, uprooted trees, logs, driftwood, and debris of all kinds were piled up by the mad waters.

For several years afterward, the canyon bottoms were a sad sight where glaring rubble had replaced lush green meadows. But, as time passed, streams were once more bordered with willows and alders and, as soil was rebuilt, herbs and grass came in again. In many places, spruce, fir, cottonwood, and even pine trees have grown up where open meadows were replaced with alluvial deposits of rubble and boulders.

How any trout at all survived this great deluge is a mystery, but the cutthroat trout is hardy and there were enough left to restock all the streams from natural spawning, which was fortunate because the territory had no hatcheries in those days for artificial restocking. Fishing was poor for several years and three boys couldn't have caught 438 trout in six hours as was done before the flood.

KNIFE-FIGHTING A WRATHY SHE-BEAR

George Beatty boasted of what he would do to a bear with his foot-long "bear knives," if attacked. Miguel Lamy was forced to give a demonstration.

Miguel Lamy was a Navaho Indian who married a Spanish-American girl and settled on a place in Indian Creek, a tributary of the Pecos. As a matter of fact, it is said that Indian Creek got its name from the fact that Miguel lived there. Miguel was not just a Navaho Indian; he had the unique distinction of having been raised by the famous Bishop Lamy, who was the Catholic archbishop at Santa Fe from 1851 to 1888.

It is not known just how the tiny Indian boy fell into the hands of the Archbishop but from the time he was a little fellow, the Archbishop gave him a home, raised him to manhood, and permitted him to take his name. Miguel simply worshipped his benefactor, whom he served as altar boy and in many other capacities, and there was nothing he wouldn't have done for him.

Miguel inherited the love of hunting from his red-skinned ancestors and turned out to be quite a skillful nimrod. In later years, he regularly worked for Skipper Viles as a guide at the Mountain View resort. Miguel's left arm and shoulder were badly scarred and back of the scars lay the story of a narrow escape from death. Miguel has long since gone to his reward in the happy hunting grounds and there is no way now to get the story of his rugged experience first hand.

One version is that, in the early days, he was herding sheep in the Pecos high country when two grizzlies attacked the herd. It is said he shot and killed one and wounded the other, which then charged him. His rifle stuck as he tried to reload, and the bear knocked it from his hands and bore him to the ground flat on his back. He raised his left arm to guard his face, and the big beast grabbed the arm and chewed on it furiously. With his right hand, Miguel pulled a big knife from his belt and proceeded to work on the soft underbelly of the bear, and disemboweled him. The bear sickened, let go his hold on the arm and shoulder, staggered away a few steps, and sank to the ground and died.

Mrs. George A. Viles told me recently that this story is not right, and she should know, for she interpreted the story many times from Spanish to English for the benefit of the parties Miguel guided on hunting trips. Mrs. Viles says the terrible scars were the result of a life and death encounter with a bear all right but that it happened this way:

"Miguel had gone hunting up Cave Creek, a fork of the Panchuela, and was standing beside a great big boulder in the late afternoon, when, all of a sudden, a good sized cub bear came around the boulder only a few feet from him. He shot it and, in its death agony, it squalled, whereupon the big, black mother bear came around the rock all bristled up and snarling and growling. Frantically, he tried to reload his rifle but the cartridge stuck, and, with his back to the big rock, he couldn't turn and run.

"The bear lost no time but reared up on her hind legs and attacked him. He threw up his left arm to shield his face and the bear sank her teeth in it to the bone. While she was chewing up his left arm and shoulder, with his right hand he drew a heavy, razor-sharp hunting knife from his belt and slashed the bear's throat again and again until it was cut clear to the bone, and she sank to the ground and died at his feet. Miguel then had to walk about eight miles to the Cristino Rivera place for help, and almost bled to death before he got there."

That, no doubt, is the correct story.

Miguel Lamy, along with his pals, Pablo Gonzales and Tony Gabaldon, built trails for me when I was district ranger at Panchuela, in 1910, 1911, and 1912. He was proud of his bear scars, which, as scars go, were indeed something to be proud of.

Mountain Picnic

Back in the sparsely populated mountain country, before the coming of the automobile, there was little opportunity for social activities outside the family circle. The stifled craving of a naturally gregarious people for normal social intercourse did, upon occasion, however, find an opportunity for satisfaction. Perhaps, the greatest of such occasions for mountain people was the big community Fourth of July picnic.

One rather extraordinary picnic and celebration took place on the upper Pecos on the Fourth of July, 1892. Henry and Mrs. Winsor, who lived at the present site of the Mountain View Ranch, sponsored the affair, making all arrangements by mail with guests who lived at a distance as there were no telephones in the area in those days. Not only were the young people of the upper Pecos settlements invited but those living on the east side of the range, twenty to twenty-five miles away, got a bid also.

My older brother, Charlie, two of my older sisters, Minnie and Ida, some of the Ground family, and Charlie Heinlen, another neighbor, went by way of the Dr. Sparks ranch, above Rociada and some six miles from our place on the Sapello. There the Sparks girls, Ada, Carrie, and Mabel, joined them to make up a party of ten. They left our place on horseback at daylight and made the twenty-five mile trip by trail, and none too good a trail at that, over the range, to the Winsor Ranch, arriving at sundown.

Of course, the trip was made on July 3, and they were all guests at the Winsor Ranch that night. Next day the big picnic and Fourth of July celebration was held on a grassy carpet in the shade of blue spruce trees where the Panchuela Ranger Station is now located. There is no record of just who was there but the assembly included, in addition to those mentioned, George Viles and others of the Viles family, Jim Bullock, Tom Stewart, some of the Gilmores, and many others from afar. It was a mighty big crowd to get together in this remote mountain region.

The feature of the celebration was a big fish fry. Henry Winsor, Tom Stewart, and one other had caught over four hundred fine cutthroat trout for the occasion. They were cooked in huge frying pans and Dutch ovens over a campfire. Can you imagine anything more delicious? It is reported that the other staple foods, pies, cakes, and homemade ice cream rivaled the trout.

All day they visited, ate, sang songs, played games, ran races, and had a wonderful time. It was a fitting outlet for the pent-up gregarious instincts curbed for most of the year. It was, indeed, a great chance to get acquainted and for social enjoyment.

Mabel Sparks and Charlie Heinlen came in for a good bit of teasing, for a romance, which culminated in their marriage some time later, and which had budded on the trail the day before, was fast and noticeably coming to full bloom.

A full day and an evening of wholesome enjoyment was indulged in so heartily that it was not soon to be forgotten. But all good things must come to an end, and by sunrise the third day the party from the east side was on its way home with plenty to talk about all the way. The trail was not graded at all, nor was it well cut out, and travel was necessarily slow. They went up past Grass Mountain, near the lower end of Hamilton Mesa, down to the Mora Flats, up the Rito Del Oso where Professor Dyche camped, and over the twelve-thousand-foot range. The descent of four thousand feet to the Sparks' Ranch was the most tedious part of the trip.

Such gatherings as this broke the monotony of isolated mountain life and the enjoyment and pleasures of them were lived over and over again in memory for years afterward. Some of those who were at this party sixty years ago are still living and recall the events with pleasant memories to this day.

TRAILING SIXTY-YEAR-OLD SIGN

The big, tall, Engelmann spruce tree which grew in a willow thicket on the bank of the stream, a stone's throw from Beatty's Cabin, died several years ago and fell across the stream. In the summer of 1951, Game Patrolman Henry Gallegos called Harold Walter's attention to a big blaze on the top side of the log. Upon closer examination, they found that seven names were neatly carved in the wood where the bark had been peeled off. That was not too unusual, for many people carve their names or initials in the soft, smooth bark of aspen trees. But the size of the blaze, about thirty inches long by twenty inches wide, and the neat carving at once attracted their attention, and when they saw the date, they were amazed. It was June 29, 1891. It had been carved there sixty years before.

They told me about it; so, when I went up there during the elk season that fall, Bob Ground and I cut the slab out and brought it home. The names carved on it were: Arthur Knaebel, then the date, June 29, 1891; below that, F. M. Wynkoop, J. G. Shofield, J. B. Sloan, W. Fayette, F. Gulden, and W. B. Hilde-brand. My curiosity was aroused and I set to work to find out something about these men and their trip to Beatty's Cabin country.

I found that J. B. Sloan had a sister still living in Santa Fe; also, that a Mr. Harman Wynkoop, a brother of F. M. Wynkoop, lived only three blocks from my office. I went to see him and he gave me the address of F. M. Wynkoop, who lives at Carmel, California, to whom I wrote for information about the trip. We are indebted to Mr. Wynkoop for the following information:

"For this particular trip, which was one of several we made into the Pecos high country to hunt and fish, we borrowed fifteen burros from Dr. J. H. Sloan. The burros were for packing our outfit but we traveled afoot. We went via the Bishop's Lodge, up the Big Tesuque Canyon a ways, then took a trackless northeasterly course along the western slopes of the Sangre de Cristo Range to the base of the southernmost Truchas Peak. Then we went southeasterly over a pass covered by a great expanse of snow to the Rito de Los Chimayosos and down that stream to Beatty's Cabin. We camped the first night in an empty cabin at Rancho Viejo on the Panchuela west, next in the opening at the head of the Chimayosos, and then a long time at Beatty's Cabin.

"Then we went up to Pecos Falls where we camped a while. Enroute to the Falls, we saw a small black bear contentedly licking salt with a group of steers. We returned by way of Winsor's and across the east shoulder of Santa Fe Baldy, and down past the head of Rio en Medio, where we made our last camp.

"At every camp except three we caught an abundance of trout, bagged an occasional grouse and wild turkey, and near Beatty's one evening, from a blind facing a deer lick, we shot a buck out of a group of three deer. We were out seven weeks and made seven camps in that wonderful country.

"Concerning the members of our party, Art Knaebel was a son of Attorney John H. Knaebel, once of the Thomas B. Catron firm of lawyers, of Santa Fe. J. B. (Bert) Sloan was the son of Judge Sloan. (He had an electrical appliance shop in Santa Fe a long time, died twelve years ago). If my memory serves me correctly, Shofield was local agent for the Santa Fe branch of the Santa Fe Railway at Lamy. Either Gulden or Hildebrand, I am not sure which, suffering slightly from tuberculosis, joined our outing for his health and was considerably improved by the trip.

"Willie Fayette probably was in Cuba with Roosevelt's Rough Riders or in the Philippines with the 31st Infantry. I was the son of Colonel Edward W. Wynkoop, who commanded, during, and after, the Civil War, the 1st Regiment of the Colorado Cavalry, which, with other Colorado and New Mexican forces commanded by Brigadier General Christopher (Kit)

Carson at Glorieta, defeated and caused the Texas Confederates to retreat back down the Rio Grande."

And so we have first hand the very brief account of a seven weeks' trip into the Pecos high country over sixty years ago. Imagine a group of seven men getting away from the hustle and bustle of high tension living today and burying themselves in the wilderness for seven weeks.

It Just Wasn't Their Time

Forest Ranger Bob Ground tells this exciting adventure story of a trip he made with my two younger brothers, Marion and Omar.

"About 1906, Marion, Omar, and I decided to go on a bear hunt in the upper Pecos country. We had two pack burros and an extra one along to kill for bear bait. On our way over from Sapello Canyon, as we crossed over the divide into the Palo-cientos drainage, the pack on one of the burros slipped and we saw we would have to repack it. It was raining and thundering, and the lightning was flashing too close for comfort. We stopped on the steep hillside to fix the pack but it was so muddy and slick there in the old burned-over area that we could hardly stand up.

"Since I was the oldest of the three, I suggested that we move on down the hill fifty or sixty feet to a little flat place to do the repacking. We did so, and had just finished the job and started to get on our horses when a bolt of lightning struck a stump not ten feet from where we had first started to repack the burro. When the bolt hit the stump we were dazed and all we saw was a big ball of blinding fire. My horse ran off down the hill and it was some time before I could get my wits together to go catch him. Marion had his hand on the metal plate on the stock of his gun and it burned his hand. Had we remained where we started to repack the burro there is no question but that we would have all been killed instantly."

By what a narrow margin were those three young lives spared! Was it a simple act of Providence that they moved, or was it just not their time?

Bob goes on to say, "Despite our narrow escape, we went on down to the lower end of the Mora Flats, where we camped for several days. We heard twigs breaking around our camp one night and thought it was a bear. Marion fired his gun to scare it away. We were out for bear but didn't want them in our tent at night. We set a trap for the bear but caught a cow instead. It was the most exciting trip I ever had, probably because we were just impressionable kids."

How Beatty's Cabin Was Rebuilt

From 1910 to 1912, the summer headquarters of the Pecos National Forest, as well as the District Ranger's headquarters, was at the Panchuela Ranger Station, at the end of the road, twenty-one miles above the town of Pecos. Perhaps, wagon-trail would be more nearly correct than road for it was narrow and rough; and, by 1912, only two or three cars had ever been all the way up over it.

Tom Stewart was the forest supervisor and I was the district ranger. We all threw in together and hired a cook and set u community cook and mess tents. The six rooms in the Ranger Station were allotted to the six regular employees for sleeping quarters. Mrs. Stewart passed away one night in September, 1911, in the northeast room. In 1910, I had the southwest room; in 1911, my young wife and I occupied it, and in 1912 our infant son shared the tiny room with us. We built a new building in the early spring of 1910, for an office building. We had no plumbing at all except that running water was piped to a hydrant in the yard, but darned if we didn't all get along fine, get a lot of work done, and have a good time.

Tom Stewart was a good worker and industrious, but he didn't like office work. The regular deputy supervisor was on other assignments most of the time and it fell to my lot to run the office much of the time while Stewart was in the field. In 1912, I did have a patrolman to help some with the field work. George Beatty's original cabin had long since rotted down to where it was not usable at all and there was great need for an administrative cabin up there in the center of the high country in which to store fire tools and a camp outfit, so that shelter, grub, and equipment would be there always without having to take in a pack outfit. The maximum that Congress would allow for building a full size ranger's dwelling had been $500, but along about that time it was raised to $650.

There was no chance to get authority to build a house up there at Beatty's and even our request for a one-room cabin was turned down. Higher authority thought that a tool box in which to cache some fire-fighting tools and emergency rations would serve the purpose nicely, so they gave us the magnificent sum of $25 to install a fire-tool box. Stewart wasn't pleased and he didn't agree with the reasoning at all. "Hell's fire, you can't sleep in a two-by-two-by-six-foot box with a lot of rakes and shovels," he declared, "besides, I, for one, want to stay out of that size box as long as I can." He didn't say what he was going to do about it but one could tell from the glint in his eye that he had something up his sleeve.

He soon bought some light corrugated iron roofing, some nails and a pair of hinges and said he was going to use the material to build a tool box at Beatty's Cabin. One morning he told me that I was to have charge of the office for ten days. Then he took Pablo Gonzales, an expert axman who had been cutting out trails for us, loaded three pack, animals with camp outfit, a supply of new fire tools, two extra-sharp axes, a crosscut saw, an adz, the iron roofing, nails, hinges, etc., and set out for Beatty's Cabin.

Three days later, I had to ride up there to see him on some important business that had come up, and found they had finished cutting and peeling a full set of logs for a twelve by sixteen-foot cabin. My saddle horse, Nig, was unusually good at pulling with a rope from the saddle horn, so Nig and I got in on the job of dragging the logs across the creek and up to the cabin site. Then I had to go back and, as I left, I asked Stewart when he would be home. "As soon as I get this tool box finished," he replied, which turned out to be about a week later.

Next time I was up there, the cabin was completed, with chinking but no mortar in the cracks, a puncheon floor, which they had hewn out with the adz, a homemade door, and roof projecting out over the front end where the door was. I think the record will show that the cabin cost $24.75. That, perhaps, was the cost of the roofing, nails, door hinges, and a couple of small window sashes. Stewart's time was not charged to the project and, if you should ever run onto an old, unfinished trail, it just might be the one that Pablo was supposed to be cutting out while he was actually helping build the cabin.

From that time on, the little administration cabin has been known as Beatty's Cabin, and by many has been confused with the old original cabin that George Beatty built on the point across the creek.

When Ranger J. W. Johnson went on the district in 1920, he built the first pasture fence and, soon after that, reroofed the cabin with heavier iron roofing. Then, in 1933, I believe it was, Johnson remodeled the cabin, put in a board floor and board sheathing with shingle roof, and made it a comfortable place t stay, although it was pretty small to store grain for horses, a good cache of fire tools, and provide room for cooking, eating, and sleeping quarters.

The increased use of the high country for recreation made it necessary to have Game Department personnel up there from time to time and the little Forest Service cabin—although Game Department personnel was welcome to use it—just wasn't big enough to meet the ever-growing needs. Therefore, in 1946, the Forest Service furnished most of the material and the Game Department packed it in and built another nice log cabin, 16 x 20 feet, with overhanging roof in front and back, for firewood, saddles, game salt, etc. The pasture was enlarged also.

These two cabins meet the requirements of both agencies, for administrative purposes, but will not be expanded beyond that because it is within the wilderness area. The Pecos high country would not seem natural without a Beatty's Cabin, it having been about eighty years since the original cabin was built.

16

at beatty's cabin
once more

July 20, 1952, and here we are, delighted to be back at Beatty's Cabin in the cool, forest-scented high country once more. Lush with tall grass and herbs, the parks and glades never were more bountifully spangled with gorgeous, delicately tinted wild flowers than now. The peaks retain their majesty and the alpine forests their luring enchantment, despite the passing years. The aspen-rimmed parks and glades are as splendid in their gala floral attire, the streams as cool and clear, the whispering breeze in the treetops as soothing, and the whole mosaic panorama as completely charming as it was when I was first here, more than half-century ago.

We came in by horseback with pack outfit yesterday from the end of the road near Cowles, where we left our cars and said good-by for a brief period to the hum of high-tension modern city life. There are three couples of us, Dr. and Mrs. Brubaker, Mr. and Mrs. Via, Mrs. Barker and I, but here it is just Doc, Ruth, Clarence, Isabel, Ethel, and Elliott. At the last minute, our old beloved camp partners, Angus and Reccie Evans, and Omar and Elsa Barker found, to their great disappointment and ours, that they couldn't make the trip this year, and what a pity, for they are all absolute tops for a trip of this kind.

We took the Hamilton Mesa trail and entered the Pecos Wilderness area soon after cars were traded for good mountain horses. Along the timbered ridge, we saw where a black bear, only the night before, had turned over many rocks in search of insects for food, and eaten the tops of angelica weed growing in the aspen thickets. A little farther on, a big-eared doe deer in her reddish-brown summer coat watched us for a brief moment from the edge of the big, open park which is Hamilton Mesa, then turned and bounded away into the aspen forest. Near a little spring on the side of the mesa, a hen grouse flew up out of the tall grass with a great whirring of wings and much cackling. That gave her secret away, and we knew there were young ones hiding there in the grass. We scattered out and one at a time four young grouse the size of quail got up and flew clumsily toward the aspen timber where the mother had gone.

All the way we admired the great variety of multi-colored wild flowers. Many of the parks and glades through which we passed were veritable flower gardens. None was more gorgeous than the horse pasture at Beatty's. The riot of blossoms and the rank mountain bunch grass reflects the beneficent deep snows of the past winter and copious summer rains which, for more than a decade prior to 1952, have been greatly deficient.

There were blue columbines and red columbines, light pink and rose-purple geraniums, vetch, wild pea, wild carrots, fire weed, great quantities of both shrubby and low cinquefoil, flax, phlox, scarlet bugler, sneezeweed, blue bells of several kinds, ball dresses *(Mertensia siberica),* comfrey, wild roses, strawberries, *Pentstemon barbatus,* and others, larkspur, monks-hood, Indian paint brush, yellow and white wild mustard, angelica weed (osha in Spanish), iris, wild onion, mariposa lilies, asters of many varieties, marigold, coneflowers, goldenrod, blue and fringed gentians, kings-crown, valerium, shooting star, primrose, little elephant, wall flower, *Polemonium speciosum,* yarrow, *Zygadenus elegans,* and many others which we could not readily identify. We failed to see any tiger lilies *(Lilium philadelphicum),* which used to grow in the aspen type in association with blue columbines.

Why did we leave the luxuries of our modern homes in the city and come back here in the wilderness to camp? That might be a bit difficult to explain to those who do not have in their hearts an inborn love of the wilderness, or who cannot hear its irresistible call. If you do have that love of remote mountains and alpine forests, and thrill to their summons, there is no need for explanation.

Perhaps, one might say there is a dual reason. One, an intense need to get away, for a time, from the scene of nerve-wracking business competition and modern high-tension living; away from the hum of motors, gasoline smell, the ever-ringing telephone, blaring radios, and nickering television. The other, a recurring passion to renew one's soul, freshen one's spirit, and soothe one's nerves by communion with nature in God's great temple. Even

Moses went into the fastness of the mountain to meditate and Christ went there to pray. Is our need today less than theirs was?

There are millions who can get along without a wilderness to visit now and then, but I am not one of them. Often a man or a couple may want, and need, to be alone for a time in remote wild places. Yet friends are man's most valuable asset and his greatest consolation in time of sorrow. Likewise, the pleasures and satisfaction of a trip into the refreshing pristine environment of the wilderness areas often are greatly enhanced when experienced in company of a few dear friends.

The trip we are now on is only one of many that we have taken into the Pecos high country. Sometimes the party is larger, sometimes smaller, and, naturally, the participants vary from year to year. As old associates drop out, for one reason or another, new devotees of the trail take their places, but Ethel and I continue to make it despite her white hair and my ponderous paunch. Never did I realize how much ten inches is until my waist measure changed from 34 to 44 inches. Ethel says the fact that she has snow-white hair and I have hardly any gray hairs at all, simply shows who has been living with whom all these years; also, that my waistline is merely a tribute to the efficiency of her cooking.

Be that as it may, we had one camp trip up here long before she had any gray hairs at all and my wasp-like waist measured a mere 34 inches, which we both well remember. Let me see, it was forty-one years ago, just about this date, the first summer after we were married. I was forest ranger at the Panchuela Ranger Station. We took off one Saturday morning and rode up here, leading a pack horse with a light camp outfit, just to look, fish, and live alone together in the pristine forest.

The old cabin had tumbled down and the new one had not yet been built, so we camped under the shelter of a clump of spruce trees. We could have brought a tent but preferred to sleep out under the stars. We had no air mattresses then so we made use of fir tree branches. We placed a pole five or six inches thick across the place selected for the head of the bed. Then we cut a good supply of tips four to six inches long, from fir tree branches, out of which to fashion a soft mattress. Alpine fir is softer and far superior to spruce tips for this purpose.

We placed a thick row of branch tips, butts down and tips leaning slightly against the head pole, then in like manner, row after row was placed, each snugly against the preceding one until the full size mattress was completed. It takes a little time but, when carefully constructed, such a mattress is marvelously soft, springy, and comfortable.

We lounged around camp until late afternoon, then fished a little while, and quickly caught enough red-bellied, gamey trout for supper and breakfast. No one could have asked for a more savory feast than those delectable, freshly-caught trout, rolled in yellow corn meal and fried crisply in bacon grease, with ash-baked potatoes, Dutch-oven biscuits, butter, and coffee. It was an altogether delightful camp there beside the babbling stream beneath the brightly twinkling stars.

Next morning we rode to within a mile of Pecos Falls, tied our horses and fished on up to the falls. Never have we had better stream fishing anywhere than we found in this brushy creek tumbling along through the deep canyon of the upper Pecos. In the mile of stream that we fished, trout were abundant but not over a foot long; on the other hand, we kept nothing under nine inches. The water was crystal clear and one had to keep out of sight of the wary cutthroats, but, if we could flip a gray hackle or a coachman into a pool without being seen, we were certain to get a vigorous strike every time, then came the fun of landing him by use of sufficient skill to keep from getting all tangled up in the brush or on a root or snag in the pool. We alternated pools and, boy, did we have fun! I do not know how many trout we released but we kept about twenty apiece to take back to the others.

We had fished for about three hours when we came to the falls, where we cached the trout and rods and climbed the steep hill to get above the cataract. There we sat and watched the water tumbling noisily down over the cliff. We picked ripe wild strawberries and ate them, then went on above along the stream but could see no trout at all. The falls were too high for trout to get up over them and no one had taken the trouble to plant any up there. Since I have been State Game Warden, that section of the stream has been stocked, thus adding five miles of trout water to the fishing resources of the high country.

On the way back, we flushed a hen grouse with a covey of seven young ones about as big as quail. We picked up our rods and creels full of trout and went down the canyon to our horses, and rode on in to camp. While Ethel cooked dinner, I cleaned the trout and packed them in green grass for the trip back to Panchuela. After we had eaten, we lay in the shade and rested for a while, enjoying to the fullest the solitude of the forest. Then, as black-bellied, white-frothy-crowned thunder clouds rolled up, we hastily broke camp and set out for home over the Hamilton Mesa trail. No sooner had we crossed the river and started up the trail through the forest than lightning flashed, thunder roared and echoed through the canyons, and the rain came down in torrents. Little did we care, for the pack was covered with a heavy tarp that shed water like a roof, and our long, yellow saddle-slickers covered us and our saddles completely and kept us entirely dry except for our hands.

Once the sudden downpour was over, it drizzled on us all the way back, but in no way did it dampen our enthusiasm for camping and fishing in the high country.

Days and nights like those, spent in the great outdoors are the times when one really lives with all his heart and soul and mind and the joyous memory of living them never fades.

Although forty-one years have passed, Ethel and I both still like to fish. Whether or not an incident which happened a couple of years before that trip had anything to do with it or not, you may judge.

One day in February, 1910, shortly after I had been assigned to the Pecos Ranger District, I rode over to the H. S. (Steve) Arnold place, on Chaparrito Creek, to take his application for a grazing permit on the national forest for that season. I had never met the Arnold family; but, at the house Mrs. Arnold told me that Mr. Arnold and the boys were over on the Cow Creek place, three miles away, baling hay, so I rode on over there.

It had been cold and there was considerable snow on the ground and, in fact, much of the creek was still frozen over. When I got to the canyon, I could see the baling crew at work at a haystack a half-mile below. I noticed someone over at the creek, a hundred yards away, so I rode over there to inquire for Mr. Arnold.

Imagine my surprise when I rode around a clump of willows and came face to face with the prettiest little sixteen-year-old girl I ever did see, standing there on the ice over a big pool in the river. The young lady was as surprised as I was, and why shouldn't she be? She was fishing for trout through the ice with a horsehair snare which was, of course, illegal. Worse yet, it was out of season and she had no fishing license, but boy, she did have a beautiful string of trout!

It should be remembered that forest rangers then, as now, are required by federal statute to co-operate in the enforcement of the state game and fish laws and, hence, they carry deputy game warden commissions. Now what would you have done had you been in my place? Chivalry was not dead; on the other hand, an oath of office in which one swears to enforce the laws of the state is not to be taken lightly. She was in a predicament and I was facing a dilemma. She courteously directed me to her father down the canyon at the hay baler. That gave me time to think and her time to repent. What should I do?

She said she didn't have the money to pay a fine, and I knew the judge would say she was too young to put in jail, so what? Well, to make a long story short, the law allows two years in which to file a complaint for a game law violation. In some devious way, within that time limitation, she was remanded to my personal custody; and, in season and with proper license, she has been fishing with me ever since.

"No more game law violations for me," Ethel says, "just look what happened to me that other time."

In 1948, Ethel and I had a wonderful fishing trip to Baldy Lake with Fred Thompson, my director of fisheries, and Mrs. Thompson. We packed in, in early July but, even so, there were still some big snowdrifts in the timber above the lake.

First thing when we arrived at the lake, we hobbled all the horses out to graze, except one, and I used him, with a rope tied to the saddle horn, to drag in some dead poles and chunks for firewood. The others set up camp. When we had enough wood in for a nice evening and morning campfire, I picketed my saddle horse in an open grassy spot, where he wouldn't get tangled up; thus, we would have him to wrangle the other horses with should they wander away from camp.

By then, it was getting along toward evening and we hastily rigged our fishing rods, each putting a different kind of fly on the end of the leader, until we should see what the trout would take. At once we found out there was no need to experiment for the gamey Yellowstone cutthroats were rising enthusiastically to anything offered them. On my very first cast with an orange body, gray hackled, woolly worm fly, a sixteen-inch cutthroat hit it kerwham! hooked herself solidly and leaped clear out of the water; then the heavy-bodied female trout headed for the center of the lake and made my reel sing as she went. When, at last, I got her run stopped, she broke water time and again trying to shake the tormenting hook loose.

Playing her was fun, but gradually, with taut line and quivering rod, bent half double, she was brought to shore. We had no landing net but, at last, she tired out and, when the runs and leaps subsided, I reached down, ran my finger through her gills, and lifted her out. The others forgot their fishing and came around to admire my fine catch, while my detailed story of the great skill it took to land a trout like that made little impression.

The lake had not been stocked during the war period and there were mighty few of the big trout of prewar stocking left. It had been heavily stocked in 1946 and was literally teaming with fine, two-year-old cutthroats from seven to ten inches long. We took no more big ones but in just a few minutes, we had a-plenty of nine-inch trout for supper and breakfast. We feasted that night and next morning on freshly caught, crisply-fried trout, and there was little desire for any other food.

After supper we sat around the lively blazing campfire, talking and enjoying to the fullest the great outdoors and the rare pure air at our 11,500-foot camp. I had stood the four fly rods up on the branch of a tree high as my head, with tips leaning against the trunk, so they wouldn't get knocked down or stepped on. I had two flies on my leader and hooked the end one solidly in the cork handle, while the other, a long-shanked woolly worm, dangled free. I got up to put some more wood on the fire and clumsily bumped my head on the limb where the rods were and knocked mine off. As it fell, I grabbed to catch it but missed; the loose hook stuck in the end of my thumb and buried itself clear to the bone.

The barb prevented backing the hook out and the eye from running it on through, and we had no pliers to cut the eye off. Now I know how a hooked fish must feel. Hook or no hook, we weren't about to start home that night with the fishing prospects for the morrow what they were. We just had to find some other way, and we did. We cut the body of the woolly worm off the shank of the hook and sterilized the hook and wound with iodine. Then Fred took a little emery stone I carry to sharpen fishhooks with, and with the corner of it, filed and sawed away on the shank of the hook for what seemed like ages of intense pain until he finally cut it in two. Then he forced the hook around in a circle until the point came out and he was able to work the barb and shank on through. Nice feeling that, followed by a mighty sore thumb but fishing next morning was worth it.

Again the cutthroats were in the mood and co-operated fully by striking hard at any fly we chose to offer them. Helmi Thompson had, up to then, fly fished very little for trout and had never before caught her limit. This time it was different, and did she have fun! By noon she had her fifteen fish and could say she had taken the limit once anyway. Ethel and I kept only ten each of the nicest ones nine to ten inches long, but in that four-hour period of fishing with various kinds of small flies, we each took and carefully released approximately 80 trout of legal keeping size. It was the fastest lake fishing we had ever done and our arms were sore for a week from casting and landing trout. Fred did about the same as we, and, like us, he took home much less than the limit.

189

We had but one night to spend this time but it was fully enjoyed, despite the fishhook, with beds rolled down, and with no roof but the brightly sparkling stars. Time to pack up and head for home came all too soon, but I insisted that we ride the mile and a half over to the rim above the head of Cebadilloso Canyon to enjoy the view which never grows old. We gazed with wonder out over the magic panorama for a time, and we pointed out to Fred and Helmi many points of interest, for it was their first time to see the Pecos high country from this point of vantage. Then, just before leaving to head for home, I rolled a rock down the steep incline and, as has so often happened before, a nice buck, half-grown horns in the velvet, jumped up out of his bed above a spruce tree and bounded off around the hillside toward the South Azul.

The next year we could hardly wait for time to ripen for another trip to Baldy Lake to participate again in some royal fishing. At last the time came, and this time the party consisted of Angus and Reccie Evans, Dr. and Mrs. Lindsay, Kay and Flo Flock, Ethel and I. We went to stay two nights this time and made our camp in a new spot on the northwest side of the Lake. The weather turned chilly, it clouded and rained a little several times, but we fished despite it all.

This time we tried everything we had but the trout just wouldn't strike. We could see plenty of them and considerably bigger than the year before but they co-operated not at all. Finally, Kay tried a tiny, No. 18, gray dry fly and with it was able to take a few fish, hardly enough for one good meal. Such are the eccentricities of trout, and the varying success of the angler. But there is more to fishing than fish, and the fact that we took few fish detracted little from the soul-satisfying enjoyment of a camp trip into the high scenic country. Around the lake, blue and fringed gentians, blue columbines, and little elephants were simply gorgeous. We all had been greatly revived by the trip and resolved to do it again at the first opportunity.

That opportunity came the following year, 1950, but, much to our regret, Kay and Flo Flock had moved to Washington, D. C, to fill a higher position with the Forest Service, and could not join us. Angus and Reccie Evans, Doc and Ruth Brubaker, Ethel and I packed in to Beatty's Cabin and, by previous arrangement, Omar and Elsa Barker rode over from their home on Sapello Creek and met us there. Truly, that was one of the most congenial parties we have ever been out with, and we all made the most of our time in the high country.

Flowers were beautiful but not so abundant as during our present trip. We took turns cooking and washing dishes, but Omar was always up first, made a fire, and wrangled the horses. One day we rode to Baldy Lake and had fair fishing and a wonderful trip up the Cebadilloso, where we saw plenty of elk tracks, and glimpsed some deer and two coveys of young grouse. The whole canyon was attractively decorated with white blossoms of skunk cabbage and the blue of the tall larkspur, both of which grow there in profusion.

Another day we rode up to the Pecos Falls and tried our luck fishing the stream above them but with little success, for the trout were all just under legal size. So we quit and rode on up above the big willow marshes and along the trail, admiring the beautiful clusters of blue *Polemonium speciosum, Pentstemon glaucous,* and blue columbines. I tried to take the party to Lost Bear Lake but again was unable to find it. They all kidded me about my woodsmanship and guiding ability or, rather, lack of them, and still do, because I couldn't find the lake.

We ate our lunch as big, black thunder clouds rolled up and. rain threatened, but it by-passed us with only a sprinkle. After lunch we rode up by the Jaroso cabin, then over the ridge to the upper Rito del Padre, where the party scattered up and down the stream to fish. Angus caught his limit, as he usually does, but the rest of us took only six or seven of the nice, active cutthroats each for that would be all we could possibly eat. It was sundown when we rode back down the deep canyon of the Rito Padre to camp at Beatty's Cabin. We had had a full day of enjoyment in the marvelous, refreshing high country.

Another day, we rode up the beautiful North Azul Canyon and through the trailless forest to charming little Truchas Lake, which nestles close up to the base of Truchas Peaks. On the slopes below the lake, where cold, clear springs came tumbling down the mountainside, the banks of vivid rose-pink primroses *(Primula farinosa)* were simply gorgeous. None of us had ever seen more profuse and beautiful wild flowers. Of course, there were many other varieties of flowers and the kings-crown and shooting stars were beautiful, but the primroses were unquestionably the beauty queens of the area that day.

At the lake we were disappointed to find that the trout had all died out during the previous winter. In the fall of 1949, I had seen them in great abundance but, evidently, the lake had frozen over too tightly that winter and with no running stream coming in, the oxygen had become exhausted and the trout smothered. This frequently happens in some of our high lakes not constantly fed by running streams of water.

We ate lunch at the lake and scouted around the hillsides, observing the gray-backed whistling marmots here and there. We also saw some little pikas, or rock conies, and their unique piles of grass curing in the sun to be stored away when thoroughly dry, for winter food. Reccie lost a valuable wrist watch and we all spent a time hunting for it, but without success.

We returned leisurely by the same route we had gone up, and enjoyed every foot of the ride back to camp. On the Rito Padre some of us stopped to catch a mess of fish while the others went on in to camp to get supper ready. As usual, Angus caught his limit, while Doc and I took only half that many, but it was enough for a good trout breakfast. The evening was spent reminiscing and telling stories of previous adventures and experiences in the high country.

On the fifth day, we had to break camp, pack up, and head for home. Omar and Elsa went back as they had come, over the old, familiar Spring Mountain trail, while the rest of us took the picturesque Round Mountain trail back to Panchuela and the gas buggies we had left there. That was, altogether, one of the most enjoyable and gratifying trips we have ever had into the Pecos high country, or any other country for that matter.

But let's get back to our present trip. After we arrived yesterday, we got a good meal, rested a while, and then all went out and fished for a while with poor luck, but managed to get a mess for breakfast. Today we rode up the beautiful Cebadilloso Canyon to Baldy Lake, where we fished and relaxed and lunched. It was cool and windy and the trout refused to cooperate but we finally got a good mess of ten-inch cutthroats. Three other fishermen at the lake told us they and several others had easily taken their limit in an hour and a half yesterday evening but trout, like women, are notional. The bank west of the lake was as charming a flower garden as one would wish to find. Isabel Via climbed almost to the top of Pecos Baldy while the rest of us fished.

We rode back by way of the Azul Canyon, saw one deer and flushed a covey of grouse. After a delicious supper that the women prepared, we had a game of six-handed samba, and then sought our sleeping bags.

Today, we rode up the Rito Padre about four miles to fish. We had better luck; Ethel beat me seven to two and Clarence Via beat us all by taking the limit of cutthroat trout. Grass is tall and headed out and flowers blooming everywhere. Mrs. Via spent most of her time painting a scene in the canyon and it came out very well.

Clarence and Isabel said they had to go home this afternoon, so we all came in by about one o'clock and had a fine trout dinner. When it came time to get up their horses, the Vias couldn't break away from the enchanted scene. "To heck with the office, let's stay and go back early tomorrow." So they stayed over.

This afternoon Game Patrolman Henry Gallegos and his attractive wife, Peggy, came up from Panchuela to spend the night and ride with us tomorrow. But, unfortunately, at six o'clock this evening a cowboy, Encarnacion Rivera, brought Henry word that there was a yearling bear caught in a trap which had been set out for a lion down by Round Mountain, so he will have to go back early in the morning and turn it loose. Turning a bear loose when caught in a steel trap is not the easiest thing to do, but Henry and Peggy will get the job done, I'll betcha.

Today is our last day, tomorrow we will have to leave this mountain paradise and go back to nerve-wracking civilization. This morning, Clarence and Isabel got an early start for home, taking the Hamilton Mesa trail. They hated to leave and we hated to see them go. Henry and Peggy left soon afterwards for their bear chore.

Doc, Ruth, Ethel, and I rode up to Pecos Falls. We tried fishing a little while in the stream and in some new beaver dams, but had little success. We rode on upstream a couple of miles and left Ethel and Ruth to fish there while Doc and I rode up through the dense forest to Lost Bear Lake. This time I found it all right. Much to our disappointment, the trout, which have been abundant for a number of years, had all winterkilled. We cleaned up a terribly dirty picnic ground on the bank of the lake that a group of fourteen very thoughtless people had left a few days before. Why so many people litter up God's green forests, I'll never know.

Back on the stream, we fished again, caught a few, then ate lunch and lay in the sun and relaxed. We tried to identify two or three varieties of little alpine flowers, but will have to look them up. In several places along the trail were gorgeous blue banks of polemoniums and clusters of blue columbines. A mule deer doe stood in the edge of the willow marshes across the creek and watched us pass, refusing to leave the spot, indicating that she had a fawn hidden in the thicket. It was in these and many other marshes that grizzly bear used to turn great areas of the sod over in search of tender roots for food.

We rode on down to a nice park on the creek, a mile below the falls, where Ethel and I had such fun fishing forty-one years ago. Today we fished again and caught a few cutthroats and rainbows, but they were much smaller than four decades ago. There was no visible change in the deep canyon, except for beaver cuttings and elk tracks here and there, but we couldn't even hope to see a grizzly bear track.

This was just another one of those wonderful, refreshing, soothing, soul-satisfying days in the Pecos high country. We are now back at Beatty's Cabin. Ethel and Ruth are getting supper and Doc is getting in some stove wood. Tomorrow we must say good-by for a time to our beloved Beatty's Cabin and its enchanted environment, but we will return.

The years have been kind to this mountain paradise. Time has wrought little change since I first saw it, more than a half-century ago, except that it is more easy of access and bears the scars, here and there, of excess grazing use. There are good trails now where there were none before; but, most fortunately, roads and the obnoxious smell of gasoline have been kept out. Both elk and beaver have been well re-established and add greatly to the attractiveness and recreational value of the region. Mule deer are far more plentiful now than formerly but white-tails are nearly gone and grouse are scarce compared to what they were in the early days. One heaves a great sigh of regret that the noble grizzly is gone—I fear forever—because the country must be kept safe for livestock. There is hope that the bighorn sheep and ptarmigan may yet be restored. Coyotes, unknown here in the early days, have invaded the area and become destructive of game.

Drift fences here and there are out of place in a wilderness area. Yet the economic situation of the native settlements surrounding this great mountain area decrees that livestock must be summer grazed here. Since that is true, the fences are necessary to make possible proper distribution of stock. Conservative grazing and even distribution of stock will interfere but little with the high watershed value of the area and its ever-increasing recreational use.

While some of us old-timers can't help feeling a pang of regret to find so many people coming and going and camping back here in the high country where we used to enjoy almost complete solitude, we know it is right and proper that they should come on horseback and afoot to enjoy the hospitality of wilderness' open house. Since communion with nature in this remote, unspoiled country has meant so much to us through the years, in our hearts we realize that others also should be helped and inspired by it.

The unusual intensity of enjoyment experienced by a few may be sufficient justification for preservation of wilderness areas, yet God knows there are millions more who should be encouraged to get out once in a while where they can enjoy the invigorating thrills and soul-satisfying inspiration of the unspoiled wilderness; therefore, let us preserve for all time a few spots with primeval conditions in their original pristine beauty and majesty for such use.

Fortunately, the back, country can't be spoiled by being looked at or photographed, or by travel horseback or afoot, and that is the kind of travel it takes for the real meaning of the wilderness to soak in. But motor roads and all the commercialization of resources and despoliation that follow wherever the automobile goes would be fatal to the attributes of a true wilderness. For the good of future generations may the Pecos high country never be so defiled.